# dirty laundry

by
rachel brenke

© 2016 Rachel Brenke

All Rights Reserved

No part of this book may be reproduced or transmitted in any form or by any means, graphic, electronic, or mechanical, including photocopying, recording, taping, or by any information storage retrieval system, without the written permission of the publisher—except by a reviewer who may quote brief passages for magazines, newspapers, and internet sites. The cover of this book may be shown on the Internet or in promoting the book elsewhere.

*On the other side of the dirty laundry is success, personal achievement and happiness. You just can't see it without taking the right actions. Actions guided in faith, commitment and perseverance.*

*To*

*Every working person who feels they aren't good enough*

*Every mother who feels they have failed their kids*

*Every entrepreneur who just wants to achieve "it"*

*Every spouse who is trying to find time for their other*

*Every person who seems tapped out of time and energy*

# Table of Contents

Introduction ...................................................................... 1

## Part 1 - Dealing with the Issues ................................. 7

Day 1.
Stress Stinks – Like the Stuff in My Hamper ..................... 9

Day 2.
Tripping Over the Piles – Something's Gotta Go ............. 13

Day 3.
Lonely in the Laundry Room ............................................ 19

Day 4.
Toppling Clothes – Fear of Failure ................................... 25

Day 5.
A Soiled Marriage ............................................................. 31

Day 6.
Stubborn and Unkind Stains ............................................. 37

Day 7.
Riding on the High Spin Cycle .......................................... 43

## Part 2 - Changing Yourself ........................................ 49

Day 8.
Putting it all Away ............................................................ 51

Day 9.
Becoming Wrinkle Free ............................................................... 57

Day 10.
Taking Care of Business ............................................................. 65

Day 11.
Staying Delicate in the Word ..................................................... 71

Day 12.
Cleaning and Not Merely Scrubbing ........................................ 77

Day 13.
Matching Pairs ............................................................................. 83

Day 14.
Undeniably Clean ........................................................................ 89

## Part 3 - What to do When the Washer Breaks ................95

Day 15.
When it Just Breaks .................................................................... 97

Day 16.
Kicking the Machine .................................................................. 103

Day 17.
The Nuts and Bolts – Fixing It ................................................. 109

Day 18.
Coming Anew ............................................................................. 115

Day 19.
User's Manual ............................................................................. 121

Day 20.
Remembering the Old While Enjoying the New .................. 127

**Part 4 - Sharing the Load in Business and Life.............. 133**

    Day 21.
    Up to Our Elbows in The Wash Tub ........................................ 135

    Day 22.
    Kidz in the Biz ................................................................................ 141

    Day 23.
    Good, Clean Friends .................................................................... 147

    Day 24.
    Mixed Load Colleagues ............................................................... 153

    Day 25.
    The Stranger in the Laundry Basket ........................................ 159

    Day 26.
    Where's Mom?! ............................................................................. 165

    Day 27.
    Sun-Soaked on the Line .............................................................. 171

    Day 28.
    Laundromat Encounters ............................................................. 177

    Day 29.
    Sharing with God .......................................................................... 183

    Day 30.
    Sharing With the World .............................................................. 189

**In Conclusion ..................................................................... 195**

# Introduction

When I embarked upon my first business, it included a husband, children, a home and a dog. I loved doing the "family business!" It gave me a great sense of pride, fulfillment, achievement and afforded lots of lessons! In fact, it was going so well, even with the learning curve we all must face, that I felt up for another challenge – my own "business business."

One thing that was certain in my new business was my primary undertaking, of wife, mother to five human babies and one furbaby, homemaker, and Christian would still be the one I loved and invested in most, but also one that moved me toward my business of another kind. I wanted and needed the blessing of my family, which I got, then it was off to the races building myself and others with the help of God-given gifts, talents and personal perspective. Life didn't stop just because I decided to launch into entrepreneurship.

Over the years, the business of family has kept its pace with events such as my husband's deployment to Iraq, a round of post partum depression and cancer…But! I am a builder. I didn't want to miss anything that was mine, or my family's, to achieve and enjoy. I pressed on with hope, guts and a renewed sense of what's awesome about life. I juggled my various businesses - family, law, photography, consulting and traveling to present seminars to inspire, encourage and direct women.

**Then I began to wonder....**

Did other self-employed women need a quick shot in the arm, just as I had so many times and still do? Thus, my idea to put together a thirty-day devotional for gals like myself – busy about the job of family which entails, among other things, laundry day! Yes, running my personal business had so much in common with sorting our laundry by type, color, quantity and water temperature that I decided to brave the over flowing hamper of home to take its lessons into the business world.

After all, laundry comes back over and over, and we conquer it again and again! Clean clothes!

**Hurray!**

And a business that is just as fresh and complete, with all loose ends folded and put away, until the next client, next assignment or next new challenge brings us another day of wash, is just as vital and quite comparable. An overflowing hamper in my bedroom looks like a small, multi-colored landfill. In the business world it looks like stress from clients and deadlines, feeling alone at the laptop, keeping the hubby well-fed and in clean shirts, getting lunches packed, parties planned and homework done with the kids and somehow overcoming that chest-clenching fear of utter failure at any given moment.

**I wasn't actually building an empire, but was attempting to keep normal on two fronts – home and family and home and business.**

I'm still here to write this, so somehow I've found a way to pull it all together and I'd love to help you find the same. I'm reminded of times, during some of life's greatest whirlwinds, when a friend or two came to offer much needed help. We'd sit and laugh, and maybe cry, as we listened to each other and accomplished the chores around the house. There were a few times we actually sorted socks, slacks, sheets and shirts and we grew and were encouraged at the same time.

As I contemplated this devotional a little prayer came to mind, actually it's a huge one, but I worked and reworked it until it began something that could be read in less than three hours. Worked and reworked…the story of our lives, ourselves, our families and the businesses we've creatively spun from the valiant thoughts in our minds to what they looked like spread out on the table and our computer screens. So here's my prayer…yours may sound a little different, or perhaps dive right into the middle of mine and say, "Amen, Sister! I'm right there with ya!"

**However, one thing is for sure – God is with us.**

He has given us the talent, drive, curiosity, strength and stamina to give this business thing our best shot. And with His help, and a few other people and things in place, that shot will be great one! I want to sort this stuff together - all that builds up, overflows, stinks, needs special spot treatment and all that comes out smelling, feeling and looking good in the end. It's laundry day ladies and we have what it takes!

*Heavenly Father,*

*Thank you for the many blessings you've brought into my life. Thank you for salvation through your Son, for loved ones that surround me, for daily provision, health and peace. Thank you for the many gifts and talents you've given me, and for people that have been a part of my journey and growth.*

*Please help me to hear you and be aware of your presence each moment. Remind me to consult with your Word and help me to understand it, since it is the lamp to my feet and the light to my path. Please help me to be about your business in the lives of others, from my family and outward to those you would have me meet. Thank you for the moments of inspiration and great ideas! Thank you for helping me build myself, and my business, in ways that glorify you! Thank you for being my business partner, coach and cheering squad, but most of all — my Father. I give each day into your capable hands!*

*Amen*

*The best business is one that keeps you inspired, challenged and fulfilled, whether you're in the office, kitchen, laundry room or café.*

# Part 1
# Dealing with the Issues

# Day 1.
# Stress Stinks – Like the Stuff in My Hamper

They say some stress is good. A few items in the hamper is good too. To have a blouse, a pair of slacks and a couple pair of socks waiting for the washer means I have the clothes I need, and I'm thankful for that. A little stress can motivate, keep me on track and remind me to structure my time to meet my family and business obligations. However, too much of a good thing is not good. It stinks!

> *"When anxiety was great with me,*
> *your consolation brought me joy."*
> (Psalm 94:19 NIV).

I didn't feel like touching my feet to the floor, but my kids were up and at it way before the usual. They hadn't accomplished anything productive, like getting ready for school, but they were going full steam ahead leaving their early morning mark on the house. I stood in the middle of the living room with a groggy head, a pregnant, morning-stomach and a ready spew of commands hot on my tongue. The dog looked at me with some mercy – I think. My only daughter would have had mercy if one her brothers hadn't already sent her into a storm of tears with snot bubbling from her nostrils. I had twenty minutes to get them packed and out to the bus. With her on my heels, I began rushing around grabbing book bags, packing lunches, grabbing the bag of chips from my ten year old and shoving apples into less than eager hands around the table.

My daughter lunged at me, rubbing her wet face across my chest, and begging me to take revenge upon her brother. Then I said it… "I don't care!" Instantly my stomach felt even worse. Her arms went limp around my growing waste-line and she walked away. I stood there with the echo of my own words screaming in my ears, "I don't care?" Where did that come from?

I leaned against the kitchen counter feeling that I'd rather be in the restroom. I was overworked, overtired and over. Just over. And I had allowed it to spill over onto my lovely, trusting, much-like-me daughter. It was time to de-stress. It was also time to do a huge pile of laundry. When you run out of clothes, you have to wash them. When you run out of patience and tolerance, you have to make a dent in that pile too. A little laundry and a little stress speak well. I have clothes to wear and a job, or jobs, to do that keep me going. But on that morning, both were over-the top. It was time to address the stench!

Look at your dirty laundry. Is there a connection between what you see, and your level of stress? Is there too much going on in your mind or on your list? There will be those times when a sick kid needs to see the doc - today, there are too many errands to run, a birthday to plan, a lawn to tidy up, a closet to sort and stack of mail to go through. There will be clients to negotiate with, contracts to sign, deadlines to meet, supplies to be bought and work to perform. Then there's the meetings…With everyone from the neighbor, to teachers, to church committees, to business seminars and not forgetting the hubby…Hopefully dinner for two and no more! And about dinner – Oh no! Everyone's starving and we forgot to take the meat out of the freezer! It exhausts me just to think these things, but the fact is we're running many businesses at once; the business of our relationship with God, our personal care and that of others. Somewhere in all of that we've decided to start still another business, and we must do it one load at a time. It is doable. We just need to breathe deep, prioritize, slow down for better outcomes and get to bed on time!

## CHALLENGE

Throw just one load into the wash and sit back with Luke 10:38-42. It speaks of Martha, who was busily serving Jesus, being a bit too busy. Read the passage over a few times with an open and honest heart. Are you trying to do so many things that you're stressing yourself and others? Remember, a little stress and a little busy-ness is good, but pile up the activity and something's gonna stink. What truly needs to be done today? What can wait? Too busy is the opposite of procrastinating. Both are unproductive and leave a trail of regret. As you meditate on Martha, and the words spoken to her by Jesus, go throw that one load into the dryer and jot down some notes. We're business gals, we're good at jotting it down. What can you take from your reading? And about that laundry… Don't do multiple loads. Let that one load dry, fold it and put it away. One full load complete! One passage of scripture implanted for growth and peace! This isn't a marathon, it's life-giving sprint.

# Day 2.
# Tripping Over the Piles - Something's Gotta Go

I'm the first one to cheer "You can do it!" to any mom who wants to run her own business or succeed in any parallel dream.

But I'm also a realist.

I recognize that some ideas are pipedreams. I found this out early on when planning and proceeding with my grand ideas about business.

Honestly, most of them were great! At times it took a little more to actually make them function than I had originally planned, but overall I had been realistic and slowly, but surely, things began to click. However, there were other things with which I had been overly ambitious and they tripped up my peace and progress.

> *"A prudent man see danger and takes refuge…"*
> (Proverbs 22:3a)

It was time to break out the spring clothes for the family. I try to do this just before Easter. I drag the bags and boxes of clothes up from the basement and sit in the middle of the living room floor sorting. We have five children to dress. I love it when I can hand a nice item of clothing down to the next in line! I carefully select which things should be kept, which are beyond future use and which can be recycled or repurposed. So, I as sat among the piles feeling fantastic about my great forethought, sorting savvy and eye for what would go with what and in who's dresser drawer, I suddenly felt overwhelmed. All the clothes smelled a little basementy. They needed to be washed. Down again to the laundry, I went. I had five piles; one for each child. A week later I had had four piles and a week after that three, then I stopped washing my great stash of kid clothes, birthed from my fantastic forethought. But! I didn't keep tripping over them as I washed the jeans, sweaters, socks and p.j.'s they wore all the time. I'd walk into the laundry room, see them over the rim of the hamper I was carrying, then trip right over them; again and again. Sometimes a collar caught my toe, or the side of my foot turned when trying to skirt the edge of one of the mounds. I began to wonder if I'd ever get those out of my way! It was time to take action – I needed to see them coming and take refuge.

A few days later, I sorted them again. I recognized the kids really didn't have room for every item I had saved and some of them wouldn't work with the cloths they normally wore and some smelled a little too basementy… I got rid of a lot of them. As I stood hands-on-hips with a heavy sigh, making decisions on what had to go, I thought of Martha, the sister of Lazarus. I've mentioned before. I can identify with her busy-ness, diligence and desire to do many great things when only a few were needed. She had been busy doing many things and trying to meet many goals and was feeling the strain. I wondered if I had been saving too much, piling up too much and then having to process the too much I had in front of me. As I sat down with my husband that night, I shared with him what I had learned, once again in the laundry room. I compared it to my huge, but well-meaning business ambitions. Could I really meet that many clients in one afternoon? Could I realistically take on another difficult project at that specific time? Could I afford to enlarge my studio space? Did I have the time and know-how to expand my services, and could I truly make that much in a month? The truth is, my piles of ambitious dreams sat and jeered at me as I continually "caught a toe" or "turned an ankle" every time I encountered them. I began beating myself up with all the undone stuff I had over-planned, over-scheduled and over-dreamed, rather than tossing those super-colossal ideas out of my way. The more they taunted me the more unproductive I was with the things I could manage. I reminded myself that my business, my parallel dream, was my second business. It needed to be just big enough, but not too big. It needed to be just stressful enough, but not too stressful. It needed to be me-sized. And as me-sized grew, it could too, but not until. Some of my business dreams sounded great in my head, but weren't so doable in reality. I learned to look at things such as timing, resources – including my energy - and the feasibility of adding things without an additional hand on board. Some of my dreams were packed up in boxes and put in the basement, so to speak, and some headed right to the trash. I still dream of expanding and improving my business ventures, but I pick through my ideas and use only what's best and leave the good behind. That way I stay on my feet instead of tripping on my nose; too much, too big, too soon can lead to defeat of the smaller, more viable and fulfilling parts of our endeavors. So I look ahead and avoid the dangers of over-extension and defeat! As for those nice, yet unnecessary piles of spring clothes in the laundry room - they proved to be not as crucial as I once had thought and they left the house completely. I still save clothes, but I'm okay if not every piece ends up in our children's bedrooms. And I'm okay if I need to toss a dream or two out with them.

Anything tripping you up?

Did you make too many promises to yourself, family or clients? Did you have business-boulders sitting around that only super-woman could move? On my most dreaded busy-ness days, I make a list of just three things that must be done. It may be to make all of my phone calls, answer all emails and place an order for supplies. Sometimes even that's too big. So I meet with one client, set up their file and sign their contracts.

That's it!

Some piles won't move today, but they'll be waiting for us tomorrow. And some need to be moved out of our way and never reconsidered. We can't be afraid to look ourselves in the mirror and say, "Girl, you've gone past the point of dreaming and put yourself into a nightmare!"

Determine to stop tripping over the same piles, the same unrealistic goals and the same gargantuan, business-boulders in your path. We can't let our sense of vision stop us in our tracks! I've been there. I'd rather stay on my feet than my nose!

- ❖ Make a list of your business dreams, from smallest to greatest.

- ❖ Sit down with your spouse, a close friend or family member and get their opinion on the feasibility of your dreams.

- ❖ Take your list to a few others – perhaps your pastor, Bible study leader or someone else in a business comparable to yours.

- ❖ Get some advice.

- ❖ Pray, get a God consult and start getting rid of those piles – things having slim possibility for success. For whatever reason, some things just aren't the best. James 4:13-15 talks about planning too far ahead, thinking we got it all understood; knowing exactly what we'll do, where we'll be and what we'll make. Planning is good for sure, but biting off too much can cause havoc within ourselves, our families and our relationships with God.

# Day 3.
# Lonely in the Laundry Room

You'd think as many people as I come into contact with each day via social media and email that I'd be overflowing with community and satisfaction. Quite the opposite! I sometimes find myself starring at the screen of my laptop feeling as if I am the only inhabit of my universe! I start to daydream about bumper stickers I've ridden behind…the ones of the "I'd rather be doing something else" variety. I'd rather be sitting in a café with a friend. I'd rather be on the escalator at the mall with a friend. I'd rather be at a playgroup chatting with a friend. Well, I'd just rather be with a friend! Or my husband, or my Bible study group, or at a church picnic, or at a business seminar, or anything at all that would give me another face to look at!

> *"Put your outdoor work in order and get your fields ready; after that, build your house."*
> (Proverbs 24:27).

When I was working a 9-5 all I could think was "I can't wait until I have no commute, no crazy coworkers and no time clock to punch!" So I quit and opened my own business. Little did I realize that with the autonomy of being a business owner also comes the deafening quiet and loneliness of working on your own. Even though I work with various independent contractors via the internet-it gets lonely. There is something to be said about having Cooky Cathy looking over the cubicle asking me the name of my nail polish color or giving me every detail of her weekend at the welder's convention.

Even though I work best by myself and "in the zone" - some days I really crave having Cooky Cathy or even Mystical Maggie around. Sure, I have the kiddos with me the majority of the time, and I love being a mom, but when I go to the studio and there is no one and nothing there to make a sound except me…It gets lonely. Ever noticed how your sounds and those of other people register differently? I can tap away on my keyboard for hours and it sounds rather ho-hum, but if I hear someone else tapping and clicking away, that's company!

Sometimes I pack up my stuff and go to the Café next door. I find a spot where the action is and settle in to think, create, work and achieve. Maybe it's the conditioning received by a mom of five kids, but I'm able to put out some of my best stuff in such an atmosphere. So, here's the question – Why have my own studio? I'm still thinking about that one.

Then I get mad at myself – This is what you wanted! This is why you've worked so hard. You get to do what you want, when you want, how you want (within reason) and enjoy the peace of your own presence. However, most business owners are people-people to some extent. They love to interact with others which makes them great at marketing, customer service and public relations. Did I say public relations? Then you realize most of what you do will be in solitude. Not public.

We know of major movie stars that seem to have it all, or at least all of what they thought they wanted, or what we may want, and they succumb to depression, drugs and other addictions. I've wondered what makes them feel so alone. Did they achieve autonomy just to see that not many where there? I'm not speaking of mental illness, just the everyday loneliness that can accompany being someplace others are not.

Being a work-at-home-mom can bring me to tears some days. I stand there realizing it's just me, there's lots to be done, the ideas come only from me; the sights, sounds and movements are mine alone. Many times I've thought of this pathetic picture - me having the privilege to do what I've dreamed of and hating it! Then I think of all the moms that would love to get a chance to do their own thing…

I know I'm not alone in this. I've spoken with many stay-at-home-working-moms who sort through the lonelies just like me. Many make those calls, lists, products and meetings all day then do their "homework" at night. Social life is an occasional luxury. The truth is we get to do what we want and it's not all perfect. And that's okay! We aren't alone in our feelings of loneliness.

Honestly, I've gone to women's retreats and prayer groups and felt more alone than I do at home sometimes. I wasn't into the crafting thing, the house remodeling thing, the block parties or the latest sale on hand bags. Don't get me wrong, I love all those things! But my thoughts were on business. How do you sell those crafts? Do you have an office in your newly remodeled basement? When the neighborhood gets together do they raise funds for a charity? Have you ever thought of having your own boutique full of handbags? So, I laugh at myself and get on with the next thing.

Honest again, I've gone to business seminars and felt drained. I should add this new technique to obtain clients, I should commit to answers all calls and emails within twelve hours like the work-shop instructor exhorted. I shouldn't feel lonely, but rather be energized with the visions of my own success. And if Cooky Cathy knew how awesome my life in the studio was, she'd be putting in her two week's notice and buying that welding shop.

Honest yet again…How many volunteers do you have running down into the laundry room eager to give you a hand? A dear friend of mine keeps a garden for the express purpose of having weeds to pull! Why? She knows there will be no joiners when she goes out to fuss over her peppers and tomatoes. Weeding gives her solitude.

Balance is the key. Lonely can be good - reflective, productive and fulfilling. It can revive, restore and energize. And who doesn't like to present to the family evidence of those lonely hours in the form of a round of ice cream cones, concert tickets, a weekend at the beach or a new car? It's about the same with that laundry. No one joins me at the washer, but when I slide a fresh stack of clean underclothes into their drawer or nicely pressed shirts into their closet, that's all that matters. And I survived the fit I threw during the spin cycle, just as I did the monotonous tick-tock of the clock in my studio.

Proverbs 24:27 tells us to get first things done first, then go on to the other things. I think of the famer out in the field. There may be others in the field, but they're too busy to chat and he's probably out there all day on some sort of machinery with his own monotony. Then he comes in to the family. I see my business much the same. I brave the business end, even the loneliness, then regroup with my husband and kids. We all had stuff to do and we were all thrilled to pile onto the sectional and enjoy the splendor of NOT being alone! And in clean clothes, I might add.

Ever get lonely with your decision to go into business for you and your family? Of course you do! It's a sign that you're a living, breathing human being with totally normal, God-given needs to connect. Think of the times you feel those walls caving in the most. Or that clock ticking too loud! Or that pile of laundry screaming at you to come do something else just as lonely! It's the same for all of us. Know you are not alone sitting in that room, lots of us are sitting in our rooms at the same time. We're together being alone!

## CHALLENGE

Plan to be lonely! What will you do when it gets over whelming? Make a list of things to get you through and back to creativity and production. Is there a special sequence of songs you can play to jerk you back on track? Can you limit yourself to a five minute call to set up a lunch date with your husband or a friend? Do you need to send flowers to someone that may feel just as lonely? Or send a quick text to say "SOS from a fellow lone-business-mom shut into her 8X10 office with nothing but the sound of the garbage truck out front!" And if a text comes back, be thankful and keep it short! If the day is just too underground and you're about to curl up in the corner – take a brisk walk and talk with God. And if you can't force yourself to renter your solitary confinement that day, it's okay, but come back fresh tomorrow! Plan to be lonely, but also plan to feel the beauty of the moments when there are plenty of arms around you!

# Day 4.
# Toppling Clothes –
# Fear of Failure

As our kids learn to walk, go down stairs and remove themselves off of furniture we find ourselves saying, "You're gonna fall!" We can foresee the outcome of their next move faster than we can yell their names in panic! We know they're gonna fall because it's a natural process as they learn to calculate and improve their methods of navigating the world around them. Generally speaking, our kids don't stop running, jumping and climbing because they got a little roughed up along the way. They will learn a caution here and there, but outright fear rarely impedes their progress. I've learned a few things from their insistence to jump off the sofa or climb onto the kitchen counter. Fear can be conquered!

*"I sought the Lord, and he answered me;*
*he delivered me from all my fears."*
(Psalm 34:4).

I got a bee in my bonnet this past year that I wanted to learn to run. A friend found that rather amusing; that I must LEARN to run. This truth is, I hated running! I could hardly run a mile even at the peak of my swim "career." I say career loosely since I'm speaking of my high school and college swim classes. But I took up running and to this day, I hate it! However, I like the challenge. I've learned a lot from it and something it taught, which I apply to business is – No one really cares if you succeed. Stick with me. The majority of people in our lives notice the various sized victories we've already accomplished. Chances are they applaud the addition of our own business just for giving it a try. But we know trying isn't enough. We want to do this thing and do it well! We want to jump off that couch and land on both feet! We want to run that race and have the sweat and the trophy to prove it!

While improving my run, my friends cheered on my progress and posted, pinned and shared my race-day photos all over social media. They applauded each time I broke through the finish line, whether I ran through, walked through or fell through it on my knees. No one yelled, "Gosh you run so slow I missed my hair appointment!" or "If I knew you were gonna crash just thirty yards from start I wouldn't have drug out the cooler, the kids, the dog and this grease-bomb sunscreen!" Nearly all those closest to me thought I was accomplishing a great endeavor worthy of fan-fare and flowers. And it's true that surviving my first 5k, without need of an ambulance, was monumental.

Back at home, where the adrenaline doesn't always flow, I watched our youngest scale the coffee table with the biggest smile he could possibly stretch across his face.

I set down my basket of laundry and watched him, but got distracted when the phone rang and one of my more impatient clients was on the other end. I had done my best with her project, but she seemed to want more than anyone could possibly give. I felt fear. I didn't want to fail her or me. Next, several emails came with pressing requests and short deadlines. I felt surrounded by impossibilities and sat down feeling numb. Then I remembered I had promised another client I'd return her call before 6:00pm and it was a little past. That jilting thought sent me running downstairs, laundry basket on hip, to find her number.

As I ran down to my files I was dropping dirty clothes on the way, and as our conversation began I was running back up the stairs grabbing what I had dropped. The call was more detailed than I thought and I found myself wishing I had just sat down with pad and pencil, as I usually do. I've learned that others watch and listen to the vision we personally craft for them. If we present ourselves as calm, capable and confident; if we tell them what we do well, and keep to ourselves the things we're still studying up on, we'll get the business we want and need. As we concentrate on what we do well, we continue to hone that skill and push past the fear to try other things.

After finishing the call with my client, I picked up the rest of the clothes that had toppled out of my control and went to the laundry room. Fearful thoughts danced through my head and some of them ran past faster than I could catch them. I found myself automatically picking up towels and socks and tossing them back onto their respective piles waiting to be washed. I felt a small sense of accomplishment just fixing what had toppled over, although I still needed to do the wash. I went back to my business list and tidied it up as well. There was so much more I needed to learn. I was sure others out there knew far more than me, and for a moment I wondered why it was important to try something others were already good at. And I wondered, "What if I never get good at this?"

Fears unleashed will topple our work loads and emotions; making a mess of both. When I watch each of our children learn to walk, I know they're gonna fall, but the end result is worth all the bumps and bruises. When I was learning to run it wasn't always graceful either, and when retrieving dirty laundry off the stairs, I'm consenting to pick up the bad stuff, put it back where it belongs and deal with it appropriately. In business, as in my personal life, I'm gonna fall. I'm glad the falls are fewer and lighter and my fears are lesser as well. My husband, children, friends and family all cheer me on as if I were acing a marathon, and maybe I am!

Think through the various components of your business. What is it that's piling up, toppling over and terrifying you? Do you need some help prioritizing your efforts to have the greatest impact? Do you need to silence your fears, get in the middle of the project and just complete the thing? Or start the thing? Or revise and regather things that have fallen by the wayside? Don't let fear stop you from what you've decided to start.

## CHALLENGE

Right now, go pile up a heap of blankets. It's a good visual. Stack them until they spill over onto the floor? Sit and study all the ways to go over, under, across or around it. It's not going to move. It's waiting for you to move it. It's the same in business. Those things that cause mounting fears are yours to conquer. If more information will alleviate your fright, then go get it. If a jaunt across town to shadow someone who's already doing it will help; set up the date. If you've over-extended your schedule or knowledge, call in emergency support! Go to God in prayer, pour out your fears and take a quiet time. Listen and reflect. Let His peace take over so your thoughts and actions are more productive. Next, climb over that coffee table, break out of the starting blocks, get a grip on those things that toppled over and remind yourself that others have learned to walk, run and master the art of the wash-day. So can you!

# Day 5.
# A Soiled Marriage

This is probably the hardest thing about a home-based-business or self-employment - keeping our marriages healthy, happy and growing. If you aren't married, there will be other close relationships you're tending, and the strain of your business can leave its mark there too. When I began my second business, after my business of family, I was sure to get full approval from my husband. We discussed the ins and outs of adding on another venture, including its effect on our time, money, communication and tolerance. We were both thorough in our approach, which meant we discussed the perceived pitfalls that lay ahead. However, we couldn't prepare for everything. In many cases we found ourselves working through things no one could have foreseen.

> *"Be completely humble and gentle;*
> *be patient, bearing with one another in love."*
> (Ephesians 4:2).

My husband Nathan has been my biggest supporter no matter what I've decided to try. Of course I attempt things I believe are actually feasible, and strive to follow scriptural guidelines in all things, so I have earned his trust. I also listen to him. Having been in the military he knows a lot about protocol, chain of command, problem solving and cooperation. Having been my husband for over eleven years, he knows me. I must also say I've been his biggest supporter. I'm not saying we're the perfect couple, but I am saying we try our best to go into things with a clear understanding of what is needed and expected. And when it came to embarking upon and branching out in business, we knew we had to set sure-fire ways to keep our relationship a priority - especially when busy or stressed.

During one particularly trying time when I had messed up my book keeping and lost a business check – both of which are not the norm for me – I became snappy with my husband and said, "Make your own dinner since you've sat around all day!" His facial expression was annoyed, and whose wouldn't be, but he didn't retort back. I scoured the house looking for that check! I couldn't tell my client I had lost it. I even dug through the pantry just in case I sat it in there while on the phone and grabbing a box of granola or cheese crackers. I heard Nathan banging around the kitchen, and the only thing in my mind was to hope he made something all the kids would eat.

Next, I searched through a pile of mail on the dining room table, and flipped through a business magazine, I had been reading, just in case I had slid it between its pages. Frantically I ran around as if a stop-watch had been set and loud buzzer was about to declare, "Time over!"

As I rounded the corner toward my room, I ran into my oldest son who was heading outside to the basketball court. He was struggling to get a hoodie over his head while rushing down the hall, and when we collided I told him to watch where he was going! His nine year old countenance dropped immediately, but I walked past looking under everything that could hide a check and in every crevice that could have swallowed it. I entered my home office and caught a glance of my full-to-overflowing inbox. I let out a groan and sunk into my desk chair. Nathan quietly walked in and sat in the love seat beside my desk. We were quiet, but I was screaming inside. He calmly announced that dinner was ready and offered to serve me in my office if I wanted to keep looking. And he was available to join the search. I was about to spout off another aggravated retort when he said, "It's up to you," and left the room. Yes, it was up to me. Was I going to keep up my lack of respect toward others and accept my own short comings?

He didn't go back to the kitchen, but into the laundry room. I heard him start a load of laundry then ask our daughter if her new jeans had been washed. Then he asked her to bring down her other dark clothes and asked one of our sons if he had anything to contribute to a "load of darks." I couldn't stand it! A "load of darks!" That described me perfectly. He was so cool, so kind and so him. I walked into the laundry to watch as he and all five kids were pitching in to smell whether something was clean or not, and to sort and chose order of wash loads. He looked up at my worried face and gave me that smile. It's the one that says, "It'll be okay and so will you."

I went upstairs and sat down to the pasta dish he had made. He sat down with me and suggested I call my client and get it over with. He was so sure she'd understand and it wouldn't damage my business reputation as much as it did my wits. I called her and yes, she was kind about the whole thing. Later that night, as I watched my husband folding basket-full number four, so many things hit me. He had chosen to take care of those things that are ongoing and kept us going, as I freaked out about a one-time mishap. He was concerned with the enduring, not with the fleeting. He was putting us first, willing to help get things back to normal so we could carry on as usual. And our usual included love, good humor, sharing, caring, prayer and joint-efforts in all we do.

As we washed dishes together he gave me a wink and said, "I didn't realize the guys make so much laundry." I smiled, happy to go back to normal communications about normal life. He had been trying to keep the lines open between us and I had shut them down. He had regarded my situation as valid and tried to help resolve it. He had also supported me by doing things I would normally do, while I rushed about the house. "Yeah, guess we all do our share of messing stuff up," I frowned. Then I asked him to forgive my impatience, anxiety and snippy attitude. I asked the same of our son.

Nathan isn't always the patient one and I'm not always the one throwing a fit or stressing out, but one of our rules is – Get back to normal ASAP and stay out of normal as little as possible. We realize the importance of mutual respect for each other, and what we do and feel. And just as communication – our words – can divided, they also are what it takes to unite. We bear with each other in love, even when it seems unbearable, and know moments once soiled can be fresh and clean once more.

Make sure you and your husband are in agreement about your business efforts. Rely on the wisdom and character of each other to weather the storms, and be honest when you're stressed and have soiled the air with unkind words or actions. We all need to clean up our messes. Have you been avoiding any conversations that need to be had? Have you neglected to give the time, love, care and respect that your loved one needs and deserves?

## CHALLENGE

Make a date with your husband and see if there's any "dirty laundry." Listen closely and thoughtfully, giving the benefit of the doubt whenever you feel about to spout. Your guy is for you, not against you. He may not be the best at expressing himself, or perhaps you aren't, but love is there. Hash it out the best way you can and get some tips from others when you hit a rough spot. We're married for a reason and nothing, not even unnerving days of business, should be given the power to make our treatment of each other – stink!

# Day 6.
# Stubborn and Unkind Stains

I want to be clear with the fact that 99% of the people in my inner circles were thrilled for me, when I decided to go into business. Well, maybe 5% of those were a bit skeptical or wondering if I had most my mind, but really they all supported me the best way they could. However, that 1% that was completely opposed truly hit me in the heart. I've heard it said that for every negative word in our ears we need four positive to cancel their impact on our emotional health. I'd say I needed at least 100 positive reinforcements per rotten review.

> *"Bear with each other and forgive one another if any of you has a grievance against someone. Forgive as the Lord forgave you."*
> (Colossians 3:13).

Anecdote I hate the phrase "Negative Nancy." I don't recall ever being referred to as such, but I could have pulled it out of my pocket to mix into the coffee cup of a close relative on a certain day at the café. I was bubbling over with great ideas for my photography business. Everyplace I looked I saw a photo-op and the quaint, little, coffee house was no exception! As I spilled over about the empty table next to ours, with its crisp, white napkins, fresh flowers and poetic "thought-for-the-day card nicely poised against the crystal vase, "Negative Nancy" let me have it!

"You have too much to do already! How can you think your own business is a smart thing to do?" she blurted over the rim of her cup. What that said to me is that I'm not keeping up with my front-line responsibilities and I'm stupid. I chewed my fresh, buttery croissant with enough force to fracture a tooth, but I remained quiet. "Besides" she continued, "You don't need to work. Nathan is a good provider. You should thank your lucky stars that you don't have to go out there like some women!" So, now I was ungrateful for my husband, for God's provision and I wanted to "go out there" when it was totally unnecessary and perhaps I should take some thought toward the women that HAD to go.

I knew I was overthinking the whole thing, but honestly I expected this person to at least pat my hand and say something like, "That's nice dear." I came home deflated and starred out the window over the kitchen sink. I was grateful. I was aware of God's ever-present care. I was sorry that some women didn't have it as good as I did. I was sorry they HAD to go out there. But! We had experienced our share of troubled spots too. My husband's medical discharge from the military was not exactly what we expected. My post-partum depression hit us all from the middle of nowhere. And what about my cancer? It wasn't fair to suggest that my life had been smooth sailing around every corner. Again, I told myself I was overthinking her words and got busy washing off the pasta maker. Pasta maker! I even made my own pasta that day! How dare she insinuate that I didn't take time for my own family! And I had every book bag ready for the next day, the diaper bag packed for the sitter's and I balanced the checkbook that night! Plus! I had the laundry done. All seven piles of it to include the brand-new, crisp, white, cotton sun dress we had just purchased for our daughter. The one with the huge mustard stain on it from an over-zealous, hot dog vendor at the block party, the one that reminded me of the crisp, white napkins at the café where I had been bumped off my happy spot the day before!

I walked into our daughter's room and rechecked the location of that horrendous yellow spot. Indeed it was gone. My consultation with the online tutorial had worked! See I was smart! When I needed to know something, I searched until I found the answer. I could do this business thing. In the sea of people I had met that week just one person was critical and unkind. It's just that the one that I thought would applaud, booed me instead. And that person really counted. At that moment I went on a mental quest to prove her wrong. I would achieve great things and make sure she knew about each one of them. For everything she seemed to insinuate, I would show my expert handling. I was smart, scheduled, accomplished, thankful and willing to donate a specified amount of free consultation hours to women that were forced to be "out there."

I let Nathan in on my thoughts and he smiled. It was his okay-honey-but-I-think-this-is-mostly-unnecessary smile. He reassured me that "Negative Nancy" was just out of the loop concerning business and deep down she supported me and perhaps quietly envied my courage. After months of successful scheduling, accomplishments, donated hours and displays of thankfulness I met the same relative again. I glowed with great things to share. And what did she reply? "Now don't get the big head. Pride comes before a fall…don't think you'll always be doing these things. There may come a time when you need to go back to being a housewife."

Oh! So now I was full of pride and I should keep failure in the back of mind for when I needed to return to being a housewife. I was over thinking again, but her words resounded. They were a blemish, a stain, an indelible mark on the front of my fresh white, sun dress or should it have been an apron?

I can't say I ever won the approval of this particular person and often times when I remember the mustard on the front of my daughter's dress I think of those conversations in the café. Their impact lessened as I grew and began seeing steady success with each of my ventures, but somewhere in the back of my mind I could still hear, "There may come a time when you need to go back to being a housewife." The fact was that I never left that job, so I was safe even with that stain in my memory.

Got a stain on your blouse today? Some of my business friends have heard much worse from closer people, such as one of their parents or very best friends. It hurts when someone who's close up and personal withdraws their support or brings in the storm clouds on our parades. Realities abound for sure, and I'd never advise anyone to "go out there" without adequate counsel and consideration, but if you must do so with a stain here or there I still say it's worth the day at the block party!

## CHALLENGE

Who's dropped a blob of mustard on your new business plan? Don't spend valuable time overthinking their insinuations or attempting to win their approval. Follow through with your original intentions and let your achievements speak for themselves, as they would have in the first place. As for the unkind blob-droppers and stain-makers, forgive them in your heart and in your prayers – on an ongoing basis. We know stains that are left untreated are almost impossible to remove later. Treat, wash, and repeat if needed – pray, forgive and pray again. The stains will eventually fade away. Next, surround yourself with people that allow you to leave your bib back in the baby's bag!

# Day 7.
# Riding on the High Spin Cycle

Most of us have heard phrases such as – It felt like my head was spinning, or I was all spun up or I spun out of control. We also know what happens when the washer is on the spin cycle and we open the lid. It supposed to stop. A spinning agitator can be dangerous, so can a business life that's too busy, too demanding, too unrealistic or too much of anything – including too fast. I briefly tried the fast lane of business and crashed. I tried the overload of business with the same result. When we're riding too high on any aspect of our lives, something or someone needs to open the lid!

*"...and God said it was good."*
(Genesis 1:10b)

I love to watch my children discover new things. It's especially fun to watch them find that they can hop on one foot, stand on their heads or do a cartwheel. I remember the time our little girl stood in the middle of the room and began to twirl round and round. I laughed so hard as she spun out into my lap with her happy giggles and wild eyes from the dizzying experience. Her brothers tried the same thing and bumped into each other until we had a pile of kids in the middle of the living room floor. Then they asked mommy to join them, while they cued one of their favorite music CDs. Oh course I obliged them and it was actually fun, relaxing and bonding as I ended up part of their heap – the one on the bottom.

A couple weeks later was New Year's. I was ready to tackle the calendar year with goals galore. Every quarter, every month and every week was chock full of advances I'd make, each surpassing the other in speed and scope. The first month went great! The second month we all got the stomach flu, which took a while to make the rounds with all seven of us, and the third month we needed to assist a family who probably got the creeping crud from us. The lady of the house was pregnant, so we volunteered to keep her kids for a few days and you guessed it. We went another round. The fourth month cooperated with my plans and I got back on track. I even accomplished some of my goals for month number five and that spurred me on to add to my expectations in the form of additional seminars, and well into month number seven I was riding high in a fantastically, productive cycle.

August came. I realize not everyone's into hot, sticky, unbearable, Florida, mid-August afternoons and really that's not my favorite time of day either, but on that one day I took the kids to the beach at the most gooey time of all. I was ahead with my reports, ahead with production, ahead with bookkeeping; I was ahead and proud of it. We hit the water with triumph!

While at the beach, one of our sons decided to start up another rousing game of who-can-spin-the-longest. I lost. He was out next. One by one each dropped onto the hot sand in a sweaty melt. We took our share of sand home in the car that day and into the house and into the laundry room. As we enjoyed our air conditioned family room that evening, we excitedly shared our day with daddy-husband. One of our sons graphically described my sandy, spin out that had sent me sprawling over one of our lawn chairs. Nathan was amused but not surprised. I'm not a klutz and not out for show, but when I'm all wrapped up in my kids... I'm all theirs and glad to be!

Nine and ten months into my knock-out business calendar a new and difficult school year started. Then the holidays came. We had out-of-town guests. On one particular morning I ran to the studio for a few hours, then back to make an over-the-top brunch for our extended family. I ran out to do some shopping then back to the studio. I had been running behind in my goals and was determined to catch up in just three or four days. In one day I made fourteen phone calls to prospective clients, set up eleven new appointments and started two new contracts. I answered over a dozen emails, processed five incoming orders and closed two files on satisfied customers. This sounds like a lot and it is, but the quantity isn't all that consumed me. It was the speed. I was rushing to meet my goals; rushing to catch up, breathless and spinning around my studio going in many different directions all at once. I drove too fast, I ate too fast, I dressed too fast and I put on my make-up so fast that I once left the house with eye-shadow on just one eye!

For the next several weeks I maintained this pace determined to check everything off my list I had contrived twelve months prior. I had pushed myself before and could do it again! I met and exceeded all milestones before and I could do even more this time around. I was bigger, better, stronger and more capable than ever, but I was totally spun.

The end of the year was in sight. I had just one more goal to achieve. I needed five new clients as the calendar turned into the new year. I got sick. Very sick. Suddenly I had chills and fever, a sore throat and body aches. My head hurt. I had the flu. But I was so close! It wasn't fair. I took some over the counter stuff that was supposed to get it over with in short order. I web searched for every home remedy anyone could concoct. Nothing helped. Conceding defeat, I dropped into bed and clutched my fuzzy blanket.

Nathan walked in with a cup of hot tea, with honey and lemon, a couple pain relievers and his great understanding. He listened to me whine as I sipped and sputtered my tea. Would you believe he was doing the laundry… Again! I could hear the washer on the lower level beneath our bedroom. I felt tired, sick, guilty and pathetic. He had the audacity to bring me my list! I had no idea what he was up to. Was he going to point out my failures? Was he going to volunteer to help me finish it off? Did he mistakenly think it was the grocery list?

Quietly he looked over my goals. He commented on my achievements and briefly sited things left undone. Then he drew a line through the current year, posted at the top of the page, and wrote in the new year. He said my goals were good and well thought except for speed and timing. Then he said something that made me gag on my orange spice, honey-lemon tea, "Since you're prone to set your bar so high, how about we reconsider the business list and reserve time and energy to perfect your spin…Just so you don't keep falling over beach chairs." My throat was too sore to laugh, but I did gag and giggle as I thought back to that day on the beach. He had lifted the lid on my spin cycle and it was time for the agitation to stop! I never repeated the "beach challenge" but I did learn to balance better and spin less!

Do you have an every-growing list of expectations that demand too much? Who are you trying to please? Remember "Negative Nancy" from day six? Don't try to please her. Are you too competitive for your own health and wellbeing? Do you expect far more from yourself than you do others? A mixture of too much to do, too little time to do it and a speeding brain that won't take "no" for an answer is a crash waiting to happen.

## CHALLENGE

Look at your list. Do you have it mapped out for six weeks when it should be six months or a year? Get a calendar and write down all the things you know are "for sures." Write in birthdays, anniversaries, dentist appointments, school and church events, etc. These are regular things you accomplish throughout the year. Look at all those achievements! Celebrate getting through two dental appointments, homework and a recital. Applaud your clean bathroom, that you called that loved one needing an listening ear and the big pot of spaghetti! Remember all the ways you've met the challenge every day! God created the heavens and the earth is just 6 days. He stopped to recognize that the work of each day was good, complete, worthy and well-done. We need to embrace our limitations and jump up and down about our achievements. They are good!

Business isn't about setting ourselves up for defeat, it isn't what proves we are worthwhile or important, it's simply an extension of the success we already are! Don't spin yourself over it. Lift that lid and know that every day well-lived and every success – the big ones and the small - are just as telling of your greatness!

# Part 2
# Changing Yourself

# Day 8.
# Putting it all Away

By now you've seen that I can get in over my head. I've made many mistakes and have applied various methods of recovery – some by chance. However, now I'd like to add another dimension to my success and survival. It's what keeps our family going; the thing that keeps my husband kindhearted and patient and me believing we can tackle anything that comes our way both in the business of family and in my personal career. I want to take a look at God.

> *"Iron sharpens iron; so a man sharpens the countenance of his friend."*
> (Proverbs 27:17)

We are regular church attenders who understand our need to lean on God. We are also surrounded by an awesome fellowship of like-minded believers in Jesus. I'm not saying we are clones of each other or that our spiritual like-mindedness means we don't have differences, but we are there for each other like a huge, caring family. When I first decided to go into business and had received the counsel and approval of my husband, we also went to our pastor and Bible study leader. We sought the wisdom of those we trusted and they offered sound biblical advice, support and prayer.

I started off working just three or four hours per week on my photography business and added gradually as we all adjusted and I gathered more clients. I offered advice to others in similar businesses and general all-around support for women trying any type of entrepreneurship. Nathan and I stayed close to our brothers and sisters at church and continued to rely on their expertise in areas we were new at. Many of them had been or were business owners. They fielded our questions, listened to our dreams and were gentle with our complaints and misgivings. We were grateful for the loyalty and the kindness of our friends and for the love and faith we shared.

What I'm saying here is that we went into business knowing we needed help every step of the way. However, I'd also like to mention the help of God. I'll admit it would have been awesome to sit across the table from Him face to face to get His take on every idea, every new encounter and every problem that needed solving. I would have loved to ask Him what I should do next, when I should expand and how many dollars to invest in getting things off the ground. Actually, He did give lots of advice through scripture and Nathan and I, along with a circle of very caring friends, would search for answers to life's daily struggles including those that came with running a business.

We met with our Bible study and prayer group each Tuesday evening. I recall a time when Tuesday was just too far away! I had gained three new clients and they wished to have photo sessions on the same weekend. I needed to build my client base and didn't want to put any of them off until later. I know now that it would have been fine if I spaced their sessions a week apart, but I was afraid to lose them and excited that they came to me! Right away I was in the thick of three clients and a learning curve. I had the drive, but fear of failure and a busy schedule, which I had not yet learned to tame, caused me to panic. I wanted to run to our study group and scream, "Help!" but I wasn't sure what they could do. It was Thursday, Tuesday was far away.

Bright and early Friday morning I called a friend for prayer. She offered to come sit with our kids so I could brain storm in my bedroom. I wrote out a plan then checked my camera, lenses, props, lights and background screens. The same friend spread the word that I was going to experience a rush and I received a beautiful show of support! Our dinners were brought to us that initial weekend of "big-time business." One of our friends cleaned and dusted my props and another tidied our den where I first began shooting. When client number one arrived, Nathan had taken the kids to the park to meet yet another friend from church. I got through the shoot with relative ease, but wondered if the truth showed. I was new at this stuff! I sent the lovely family of five on their way and in walked another friend with lunch and my favorite, fruit smoothie. She listened to my nervous and excited chatter then left in time for me to get ready, get set and go again!

The next shoot went well although the little guy I was working with was having a grumpy day. I smiled, tickled his nose with a feather, pulled out all my best silly voices and danced around the room trying to get a smile. Instead I got pouty lips and whimpers. Yikes! I had done all the mom-things I knew and I'm a pretty upbeat mommy. I felt fear grab me by the gut. I wasn't going to do well. I was gonna let this family down and mine too. I started praying in my heart. I asked God for something, anything I could try to get this sleepy, grumpy, three-year-old to smile. An idea came to me that one of our friends had shared before prayer time the previous week. I took the feather and began tickling the nose of the little one's parents; first his mommy's and then his daddy's. This may not seem so brilliant except that they had started arguing about scheduling so close to their son's naptime and I came at them by surprise! At first I wondered if I was about to lose one of my first clients. However, they both responded and soon they and my subject were smiling, then chuckling and I got some great shots of sparkling blue eyes and happy grins! As they left the house I felt I had scaled Gibraltar or at least kicked one into the soccer net! The next sitting would be the following day. I needed to chill! I sat with my laptop looking over and picking through the photos I had just taken. Some were good and some were very good and a few were just rotten. Nathan and the kids came in and looked over my shoulder.

The next day I got through the engagement session and again looked immediately at my work. By bedtime I had worked a total of thirteen hours that day, editing and grouping and readying proofs for my clients. I was too excited and again too nervous, to let things set. It wasn't long before I kicked back and relaxed after a photo shoot and felt it was reasonable to space my client sessions. But one thing that didn't change was my need for ongoing love, prayer and support from our circle of Christian friends and family.

I also continued to pray on the spot whenever things didn't seem to be going well. There was the time I dropped my camera while capturing the perfect pose and the time I forgot I had booked a session and met my good-natured clients at the door in my p.j.s. There was also the time I misplaced a contract and the time I proceeded with a shoot although I had puked my guts out just hours before. That was the time I was begging God would to keep them safe from my virus and He did! It was also the time our pastor's wife showed up with a pot of homemade chicken-noodle soup!

I learned early on to ask for help, to accept it even when I didn't ask but honestly needed it and to call upon the Lord at the drop of a hat or a camera. I learned to allow others to help me put things away. Sometimes that meant my fears, my depression or my frustrations. At other times, it meant my props, folders and boxes of orders. And yes, at other times it meant dishes and laundry. All neat, clean and out of sight. I have been in business for several years and I still call prayer parties, ask for guidance, thank God and tickle noses with feathers.

When I started my first business I was somewhat afraid to ask for help. After all I was asking for something extra, above and beyond my already wonderful friendships. I didn't want to pester people and I wasn't sure how much help I needed. Have you put meaningful thought into who and what you need to continue forward with success? Do you have a down-day plan, a rainy-day plan and a work-party plan? Do you have open communication with God and others so you can bear your heart and receive the help that's needed?

## CHALLENGE

Get vulnerable. Call for help and let others know you're approachable to come to their aid. We can't build our families without the nurturing force of those who love and care about us and we can't build our businesses without them either. The best comrades are those who share our faith, comparable lifestyle and reliance upon the Word of God as their guide to all of life. Who do you know that fits such a description? Allow them to sharpen you and your countenance as you stride along together!

# Day 9.
# Becoming Wrinkle Free

They say some people more easily forgive others than themselves. Then there are those who excuse themselves yet blame others. I say we need to treat others and ourselves with the same respect and care, and of course this is a biblical principle. This applies to all areas of life including business. I made lots of mistakes that affected others, both my family and clients. I did my best to make amends on all counts. This also meant making amends with myself! The end result is peace for everybody – even our neighborhood party people!

> *"Do to others as you would have them do to you."*
> (Luke 6:31)

> *"Love your neighbor as yourself…"*
> (Mark 12:31)

When I first started business consulting my mail came to our house. Every time I got a piece of mail from a prospective client I nearly skipped back to the porch! I was doing this! I was in business. It was real. Nearly all our neighbors knew what I was up to and would ask how it was going. And mostly it was going great – but not always.

One of our neighbors enjoyed throwing parties. It seemed they celebrated everything. I'm all about social gatherings, but not when their guests block my mailbox and prevent me from getting important things like that check I needed or that book I ordered on how to market my best features! I looked out the window to see if the candied-apple, red Lincoln was still cozied up to my mailbox. The mail truck would come at any minute. I busied myself in the kitchen with one ear toward the front of the house.

It was lunchtime. All five of our children sat around the table munching made-to-order turkey sandwiches, baby carrot sticks and apple slices. Then they dove into their homemade, lemon-lime popsicles. Feeding five kids takes time. It was time enough for the neighbor's guest to move on, and who has a party at noon on a Thursday? Next, I wiped little faces and hands and we went out to play so I could watch that mailbox! I'd like to say that the neighbor's guest left and we got our mail, but that's not what happened. So, with entourage of five, I went over to tap on their door.

I calmly explained that I was expecting important business materials and had not received my mail twice that month due to their guests parking in front of my mailbox. Then our four year old blurted, "You made my mommy mad!" I patted his head and "shushed" him then went back to my highly-animated, explanation of grief. "You are a bad neighbor," my little guy blurted again, "You are not nice!"

The neighbor suddenly looked annoyed and angrily said he'd make sure it never happened again. Then he abruptly shut his door on us.

At that point all of my kids had something to say; from why was he so upset to maybe we should bake him some brownies to help him feel better. I second guessed my actions. Maybe I should have had Nathan go over, or left a kind note on the neighbor's door begging for clearance in front of our house, or maybe I should have just let it go and went to the post office to pick up my mail. Maybe I shouldn't have taken all the kids. Maybe I should have taken the dog instead. We made the brownies.

Later that evening Nathan and I went over with the plate of double-chocolate, walnut brownies. We were invited in and Nathan explained our dilemma. Then I offered an apology for the various remarks heard earlier that day. The neighbor was gracious and forgave our part of the awkward situation and sincerely pledged to keep the way open from then on out. The next week we missed our mail twice.

This same thing occurred throughout the summer and nothing in me wanted to bake another batch of brownies! It was a particularly trying week. A client didn't pay as agreed, I lost another one due to an misunderstanding of services available and my oldest son received a slight injury at the park. I was stressed and again had missed an important document through the mail. I drove to the post office in a huff.

I had plenty of words for the client that didn't follow through with payment and I was sure I had explained all services available at my photography studios. My son's three stitches to his forehead bothered me, as did the dogs gastro disturbance on the kitchen floor and our daughter's melt-down over her missing princess bracelet, but the root to my dismay was all about the neighbor! Or something else…

I'm the kind of person that wants everyone to be happy. I'll sometimes go to great lengths, further than I should, to make sure everyone has peace, harmony and a positive disposition. This has carried into my business endeavors and while it should – client care and appreciation – it has also caused me to blame myself and hold grudges about my failures! Yes, I've held grudges against myself.

There was a time that if I worded something wrong and it caused a misunderstanding I not only improved my script but tried to avoid that type of situation again – at all costs. This meant I shied away from anything near that previous experience. I couldn't forgive my slip-up. I was embarrassed, self-deprecating and afraid of repeated failure. I would tell myself how wrong I had been and give the other guy or gal the benefit of the doubt, and the upper hand of innocence. It didn't matter if they could have helped to catch the error, had given me incomplete information or didn't keep their word. I was the business consultant, the overseeing lawyer and the photographer that owned the studios other photographers were using. I held myself responsible because someone was not completely happy – no matter what.

This thing with the neighbor was really getting me down. This time I knew I had done all I could and I wanted him to do all he could. I wanted him to consider me and make me happy! It was in his power! If I had the power to make someone's day, you bet I would! If I had the chance to help someone succeed in their business efforts – I would do it! I wanted him to be like me! In actuality I wanted him to be like Christ! That's what I was trying to do. Treat others as I wanted to be treated. Love my neighbor as myself. It worked for me, why not him? The short answer was he wasn't interested in biblical principles and I was. And he wasn't interested in my business!

I sat alone in the porch swing in our back yard. Moments alone can be rare in my life and honestly I'd rather be surrounded with people much of the time. But I took a few minutes to quietly reflect and listen to the birds sing. I looked down at my capris – they were wrinkled. That's what happens when I'm too tired to fold the laundry and it sits in a heap on the chair in our bedroom for a few days. I started to chide myself. Then I saw a dark blue SUV pull up in front of mailbox and go to the neighbors! Forget the wrinkled capris! I jumped out of my swing and made a bee-line for the neighbors. This had gone on way too long!

As I made my way across the lawn the neighbor was heading out to meet his guests. I stopped as he directed them to park away from my house, then turned and saw me and smiled and waved. Instantly I felt silly. I waved back and returned to my swing. I looked down at my wrinkled pants again. Well, nobody's perfect. And it was ok that looked like I had been too busy to tend to the laundry as I'd like. The birds were still singing and I didn't hold a grudge against myself or the neighbor. It's not like that one day on the swing cured all struggles within and without. But since I'm a photographer I went in and took a picture of me in my wrinkled capris and posted it on my social media and in my office. Wrinkled pants remind me I'm human and so is everyone else. I added just one prop to the photo. An iron! To be wrinkled is human to use the iron is divine!

Do you take note of all your mess-ups and shy away from that area again or from fixing it due to feelings of inadequacy or failure? There may be something on your mind right now that screams at you about yourself or someone else. Are your pants wrinkled? Your shirt?

Your thoughts? Maybe you've made a business mistake and there's an unhappy client in your life. You need to iron things out.

## CHALLENGE

If you are a compulsive "keep everybody happy girl" or an "I can't do the slightest thing wrong girl" or even an "I'm gonna pretend this didn't happen and look the other way girl" -get out your iron! Put on your favorite piece of clothing - done wrong! Yep! Your favorite top, pair of pants or dress and stand there wrinkled. Remember we are instructed to love ourselves just like that. We love our "look" in our favorite blouse – our best person –

even when wrinkled! We're to show the same love to others in their estate. Just as Jesus did for us.

Now go get the iron and hold it hold up like you mean it! Snap that picture. Post it someplace and commit to love yourself more, and the other person too. Iron out whatever you can lovingly, gently, and with attention to detail. Then let it go until the next ironing day!

# Day 10.
# Taking Care of Business

As I mentioned at the beginning of this devotional, my first business is that of family. And that includes me! I'm important to a lot of people and need to be just as important to myself! My emotional, spiritual and physical needs must be tended to; when I'm in good condition, so are my family and my businesses. I try not to take my bad hair days, feeling less than worthy days and thoughts about not having had a decent work-out into the office. But I do want to take all my good stuff there! And I've found I must deliberately make all that good stuff happen!

> *"He stretched out and fell asleep under the shrub. All of a sudden an angelic messenger touched him and said, "Get up and eat." He looked and right there by his head was a cake baking on hot coals and a jug of water. He ate and drank and then slept some more.'*
> *The* LORD's *angelic messenger came back again, touched him, and said, "Get up and eat, for otherwise you won't be able to make the journey."*
> (1 Kings 19:5-7)

Let's talk about postpartum depression. Since our first business is the hubby and the kids we need to remember what we already know about life! If you've had children, or have helped a new mom get through the recovery and transition time of a new baby, you know there are many steps to work through. That may mean losing some weight, doing something with your hair, other than pulling it back from the direct shot of baby puke, and resting while others pitch in with the cooking and cleaning. It may mean all that plus deciding you need tons of encouragement from close friends; someone to listen to you, pray with you and a new mom devo on your nightstand. It may mean all that plus professional help when you're so overwhelmed and bewildered that all of the above is nice but not enough. The business of life can get crazy for anyone and for us ladies it has its cycles and stages that cannot be denied. Now what about that postpartum depression?

I have five children. I love being a mom and I think most would agree that I do a great job at it! I'm a fun mom, a creative mom, one that laughs with her kids, chasing them with my best "gonna get you" warning and am just as fast with the tickle machine as I am with warm, soft hugs. I can easily deal with their doctors, public school and Sunday school teachers and all their friend's parents. I read to them, train them not to lick their fingers and teach why we don't peel our clothes off in a trail down to the laundry room. And I coach their sandbox play dates right along with their sibling interactions concerning anything from who took who's library book to who grabbed the biggest slice of cake…again…and who needs to ask forgiveness for spilling their entire twelve ounce lemonade on their sister's favorite plushy. I do a lot. I know it and I love it!

When postpartum depression struck, it was not only one of the worst times of my life but I was also shocked that it was happening to me! I loved my babies – all of them. My husband was a true hands-on dad and I had tons of supportive friends and family around me. So what was going on! I had to learn about and accept things like hormonal fluctuations, feelings of overload, fears of never catching up or never being enough or that life had finally wrestled me to the mat and I was never going to get up! I fought feelings of giving up since it seemed I was not going to be let up by this fierce depression. There were days I didn't want to eat, nights that I couldn't sleep then others when I didn't want to wake up. Ick! Just thinking about it gives me the creeps! But also it reminds me about being victorious! It took a while to crawl out and up to where I had been previously, but it did teach me a few things. I learned of my own importance. How my needs were valid. How I needed something to look forward to and goals to accomplish and I needed to tend to me, not just the family. I needed good nutrition, a slowly building work-out plan, plenty of rest, plenty of helpers and when I needed to sob through an entire box of tissues it was okay. And when I had my perk it was time to enjoy it to the max. I also learned about quiet times with the Lord. I took them more frequently; reading through Psalms dozens of times, praying and journaling my thoughts. I could look back through my previous entries and see how I was progressing in strength. I kept all my counseling and doctor's appointments and allowed them to monitor me.

Nathan and I also saw our pastor and his wife. They came to our home offering their arms, hearts and ears to both of us.

Postpartum depression is its own monster but everyday life presents similar needs. No one can sleep for us, eat for us or exercise for us. And no one can think for us, pray our prayers and journal our thoughts. No one can carry on our relationship with God, others and ourselves! Life is work! So, our first business is keeping us in top shape for daily functioning. We do these same things for our loved ones - and sisters, we are one of our loved ones!

I remember one day in particular when two friends came over to work me over! One did my hair as I sat up in bed. The other one painted my toenails! It was beautiful! Then we read a devo for new moms and shared some thoughts and prayed. Then they spread out a quilt over the top of my duvet and we had a picnic! Those were the best crumbs in the sheets I've ever had!

So this devotional is entitled Dirty Laundry. Where does it fit in this particular day's reading? Sometimes we don't want to talk about our most basic needs any more than we want someone to go through the family hamper! We don't want to air our dirty laundry. But all of us need to eat, sleep, go potty, talk, be understood and have a peaceful and restful existence! We all need to be loved, assured of our place in this world, confident about our daily bread and that if the scales say something other than "You look awesome!" that we can cope.

Elijah was going about his business of being a prophet of God. It got him into trouble. He stretched out on the ground and wanted to die! God didn't remove the circumstances but said everyday stuff like – "Hey! Time to grab some breakfast!" and then again "Dinner time!" When we take care of our first business we'll have what we need to face our other businesses with confidence. First things first – always and in every way!

Think about your best days, when you have lots of energy, loads of creativity and a calm disposition. Wouldn't it be fantastic to have that more often than not? If you've been neglecting to care for yourself, or your other loved ones, it's time for an evaluation. We can't carry on well in our daily lives with blatant or unintentional neglect, and to add on a business can make things spiral out of control. We can be strong, capable and successful for our families, for our clients and for ourselves when we carefully construct and execute a personal care plan. Ready to make one?

## CHALLENGE

Think about your best days. What made them "best" and what preceded them? Think about your worst days. What set them up for the worst? Try a little self-discovery exercise. For one week jot down whether or not you had proper meals, adequate water intake, rest, exercise, quiet time and prayer. Make mention of any social activities or lack thereof. Track yourself to get to know yourself! Sometimes we are on automatic and don't realize we've only had a bagel and coffee and it's 1:00pm or that we haven't spoken to our closest friend in over a week! And remember walking the dog for 30 minutes counts as exercise as does chasing the kids around the backyard and intentionally running up and down to the laundry room to retrieve just one item at a time! Brainstorm with your hubby or a close friend and get their perspective on how you can revamp your days and nights for optimal health and well-being. You may need to take the TV out of your room or swear off your social media thirty minutes prior to bedtime. You may also need to set aside a day for a picnic, even if it's in your bedroom, and another day to feed the ducks and another to hear the symphony. Refresh every area you can and put your business under new management!

# Day 11.
# Staying Delicate
# in the Word

The delicate cycle is for those things that need a gentle touch. That's where we put our pretty things, our special things and things that just can't take the beating of the agitator at regular speed and duration. I have horror stories of missing a lacy and expensive item and discovering its demise in with the sturdy cottons and denim! The most tragic was a vintage blouse with a high lacy collar, lace inset bodice and long, lacy sleeves. It was for a special event – sort of a throwback to the Victorian era – and I ruined it BEFORE the event! It was one of kind that I had found in an upscale, vintage thrift shop.

> "...We have different gifts, according to the grace given to each of us. If your gift is prophesying, then prophesy in accordance with your faith; 7 if it is serving, then serve; if it is teaching, then teach; 8 if it is to encourage, then give encouragement; if it is giving, then give generously; if it is to lead do it diligently; if it is to show mercy, do it cheerfully."
> (Romans 12:6-8).

Some of my girlfriends thought it would be fun to have a Victorian style brunch out in one of their rose gardens. We hadn't been together for months and had lots of catching up to do. The last time we gathered we did a Mexican theme. We were all small business owners and our time was at a premium. When we did something, we did it big. It was actually part of our personal care plans to gather once a quarter. This time we hit the vintage clothing stores in search of that perfect blouse, hat or ankle-length skirt complete with petticoats. Some of us were gonna do the gloves too! What fun!

The week before our late summer brunch, I had everything I needed. I was ahead of schedule, as I like to be, and modeled for our family. I walked into the living room to much applause! "You look just like a princess," my daughter squealed. Nathan snapped a few pictures with his Iphone. One of our sons jumped up, bowed and took my hand to lead me to my recliner. I felt lovely! I had chosen a pale blue, full skirt, no petticoats for me, a white, lacey blouse and a pale, yellow hat. My shoes matched my hat. My delicate handbag matched my skirt. I had to giggle at myself! No way could I romp around after the kids or go meet a client in such a "get-up" but for that time I was in character and happy to be so.

Tragedy struck when I noticed a small stain on the cuff of my new blouse. It looked like it could be removed so I tossed it on top of a pile of laundry. The wrong pile! It went through a hot, regular cycle with a bunch of gym socks and towels! It came out misshapen and with a couple of tears in the bodice! I went from thrill to defeat in a matter of minutes. I sunk into the same chair I had just sat in to smooth my skirt and pose for my husband, but this time I choked back the tears. That blouse was one of a kind!

It was unique. There was not another like it in our entire county. I couldn't replace it. I would have to go back on the hunt to find just the right one to accompany my skirt and hat.

After searching for days, I found something that would work but it wasn't as lovely. It had a high, lace collar and lacey bodice but the sleeves were too full and plain cotton. I got the same cheers and applause from my family and my friends loved it, but I knew it wasn't what I had intended. It didn't feel as "me" as the first one. These feelings struck up a conversation at the garden party. We talked about our own uniqueness. None of us were engaged in some previously unheard of business. I was business consulting, providing legal services to photographers and heading up my own photography business. My friends were hair stylists, caterers, freelance writers and a nutritionist. One of the caterers was considering her own café. Although none us had decided to invent something no one else had ever tried we all provided our own stamp and persona to what we did. The reason we could do this was because each was fashioned according to God's plan for us as individuals. Each one of a kind. Sure there are lots of business consultants, lawyers and photographers, but they aren't me and don't do it exactly the way I do.

We also talked about keeping our connection with the Word of God so that we don't lose sight of who He is, who we are and what's up in the world around us. Just as we keep savvy about business trends and personalities, we need to keep abreast and sensitive to what God wants us to know about life. This also helps us to know how to pray for each other and our families and how to deal with the bumps, hurdles and conflicts as we conduct ourselves in business. It also keeps us encouraged and reminded that no matter what – whether good day or not so great- we are totally loved and supported by our Heavenly Father!

When I meet with a client or teach a business seminar, I want each one to walk away knowing their particular strengths and personality bents. My desire is that each woman leaves valuing her one-of-a-kind contribution to the career of her choosing. This is what God intended. He gave us all life, created us in His image, then He chose the right gifts and talents and personalities for each of us. He made many teachers, but when we add in out true selves and cultivate our own characters, we have a teaching method, style and presentation which reflects as differently from others as do our finger prints.

When it came to our pieced together outfits that day, more than one of us had a similar skirt, yet they all looked different when we put them on. Some of us were tall, others shorter, some chose dark colors and some light, and the gamut of accessories gave mention to our own style and imagination. I paired white and pale yellow with my muted blue skirt, but one of my friends took a similar blue and jazzed it up with red and purple! We both looked awesome! I would have looked a bit "off" wearing her combination as she would wearing mine.

Accepting who we are with gladness can be difficult. Whether among family and friends, church groups and school groups, we should stand out as a testimony as to who God made us to be. This is the same in business. There's no need to try to duplicate someone else. We already have THAT person! This world needs OUR person!

The next quarterly gathering of friends took us to an outdoor flea market, lunch at one of our friend's new cafés and a stroll down a historic section of town where we took in an art show. The theme was "Fun in the Sun." I wore a hot pink sun dress with a straw hat and handbag. My sandals were pink and beige. One of our friends wore capris and a sailor top; another wore a jean skirt and skinny, ribbed tank, two others wore khaki shorts, one with a white, eyelet blouse and the other with a printed tee which read – "FunShine!"

Who are YOU? Do you know? First you are a unique woman created in God's image to know Him and enjoy living out the destiny He has for you. But before we can walk something out we have to know our own path. If you're already in business, or thinking about going into one, that probably tells a bit about whom you are. Next, your choice of business is another indicator. I wouldn't choose to be a caterer, but my catering friends wouldn't choose business consulting or law. The Bible speaks of God-given gifts, within those there are many facets that determine our best choices to pursue.

## CHALLENGE

Read through the Bible passage in Romans 12. Do you see yourself? Ask a few people, who know you well, to see if they can pick you out of the list. Take one of the spiritual giftings evaluations on the inner net or purchase a book and take theirs. If you know someone similar to you, see if you can connect and learn from each other. Understanding yourself as much as possible is a super great way to live and plan your life. Invest some time in learning about the gifts and personalities of those around you; it will help at home, in business and everywhere else you interact with people. Be you, there will never be another one!

# Day 12.
# Cleaning and Not Merely Scrubbing

I don't know about you, but in my busyness, distractedness, tiredness and sometimes haste I have spot treated and scrubbed a nasty stain from a piece of clothing, then not thrown the article in the wash for a complete cleaning. That usually means it's sitting on top of the dryer all ready to be cleaned, not merely spot scrubbed. And sometimes I've found I have to scrub it again before putting it in the wash! Have you done that?

> *"Therefore as you have received Christ Jesus the Lord, so walk in Him, having been firmly rooted and now being built up in Him and established in your faith, just as you were instructed, and overflowing with gratitude."*
> (Colossians 2:6-7).

With five children, and their various pursuits, I'm sure you can imagine the type of laundry sitting around waiting its turn. We have a soccer player, a ballet dancer, two dirt diggers and one still learning to direct food into his little mouth rather than on his shirt. As a photographer, I have an eye for what needs fixing, correcting and straightened up a bit here and turned a little to the right, there. I see every spot and everything out of place. My clients rely on me to ensure they have a spotless and professional photo shoot. My family...Let's say I'm sometimes, unconsciously putting them in frames.

Our two dirt diggers have a blast out in the back yard and really I don't mind the dirt! I've enjoyed many hours watching them create cities with their die-cast, front-end loaders and bulldozers. However, there are times they've brought in more than dirt. There was the time they were knees-down into a berry bush, the time they discovered a squished caterpillar on one of their shirts (don't know how that happened) and the worst of all – when one of their bottoms found what the dog had left. Yup! I can hardly stand to think about that one. So, laundry stains can get interesting in every sense.

I'm happy to report that the incident with the doggy stuff was tended to instantly, correctly and completely! The one with the berries did not. It had been a long day that seemed like two. I had answered a round of emails, gotten the older kids off to school, worked-out, completed 4 hours of photo processing, one hour of consulting, meals for the kids at home, spent two hours educating myself about business, another hour photo processing, picked up the kids from school, homework, playtime, dinnertime, family time, bedtime and finally, checked email again. Somehow Nathan and I had shared a few minutes and the house was clean as we dropped into bed. But! The laundry was not clean. I had treated the deep, purple, berry stains from the knees of two pairs of light blue shorts. Believe me, I didn't worry about it! I was glad to shut off the lights.

The next morning I started our usual routine then took a quiet time. I read about getting serious when it came to my spiritual life, in all its facets. That meant how I ran my day, tended my family and developed my businesses. Did I allow the spiritual part of me to permeate all those other areas? My personal, spiritual path meant reading and meditating upon a short Bible passage each morning and keeping an ongoing list of things I was thankful for and requests I was taking to God in prayer. It meant meeting with fellow Christians throughout the week and listening to Christian music when driving. Just stuff like that. I was pretty god at navigating my walk as a believer in Jesus.

Next, I thought about my family. Nathan and I read a Bible story to the kids before bed on most nights. We all went to church together and the kids loved Sunday school and Vacation Bible School in the summer. We prayed at meal times and readily discussed biblical principles as they applied to the various stages and interactions of our young family.

Then I thought about the way my spiritual-self entered into business. I certainly upheld godly ethics in all I did. I was fair, honest and genuinely sought to encourage and build or serve and deliver to each person that came across my path. Most of my business associates knew I was a Christian, not because I was preachy but by my demeanor and sometimes my jargon. When something is real, it just slips out!

Since I'm a goal oriented person, a forward moving and progressive person, I regularly take stock to see if I could improve the course of my spiritual life. I don't want to just "scrub out the spots" as they occur, I wanted to make sure I'm all-over, clean and fresh. And when we do the same things over and over it can get dull, so a once-over evaluation is a great thing!

The need to do a personal inventory came when a conflict arose with an acquaintance. It was nothing big, but I didn't want to just scrub the spot. I wanted a good all-around relationship with this gal. It was so clear to both of us that we would mutually benefit each other personally and in business, but we needed to work at it a bit. We did the work and now our relationship is growing and is a real blessing!

I decided to do the same thing with the Lord. It's definitely a HUGE benefit to be His child! And I wanted to be a daughter He could count on to be a light to others and to spread His love all over the place! In order to do this I added a few things to my personal care plan. I left my ear buds out when taking a walk or working out. And I turned off the radio when alone in the car. Sometimes I was just aware of His peaceful love and care around me. Sometimes a grand idea popped into my mind and I knew He was behind it! Other times a song played in my thoughts and it encouraged and uplifted me so that I passed it on to others that day.

I'm a lot of things to a lot of people, but first I am a child of God. How awesome is that! I keep things right between He and I and that makes the difference in all my relationships and all I do. He wants us all of us, because He has so much to give! He doesn't just want to scrub out our spots – although spots will come – He wants to keep us line-dried-fresh all over, all the time!

Is it time for you to check out your path? I say it's a grand adventure in progress! I think most of us are morally fit and doing fine as it pertains to this world. Yes, we'll get a spot on our knees and need to scrub it, but an overall checkup is good too. Do you have business plans, but not so much in the area of spiritual plans? I remember a time I was big on business, mainly because I was a major novice, and just sort of cruising spiritually. However, as I built a better spiritual plan and grew as a Christian, even my business did better! It just happened. As I focused on God, He became my biggest business partner. I'm sure He has directed my steps. I've never regretted plotting a spiritual plan for progress. It's the best investment I've ever made.

## CHALLENGE

How can you include more spiritual time and focus into your life? Are there wasted moments you could recapture to make sure you're over-all clean and growing, not just spot-checked when needed? This is where journaling may come in handy again. Maybe writing out your prayers of thanksgiving or just jotting down something for which you're thankful at the end of the day. These things can help increase your awareness of God's presence and His direction in your life. Do you need to add prayer before diving into your day, or at the end of it for a good night's sleep? Think about how much time you spend in the various areas of your life. How much of it belongs to you and God? Believe me, we all need Him on our path and He wants to be there!

# Day 13.
# Matching Pairs

Having and following a personal care plan will help ensure that we running at peak performance spiritually, physically, mentally and emotionally. It makes sure our relationships are what they should be with God, our families and friends and those we come into contact with in our many paths and circles. However, there is a matching pair that needs to be in the forefront of our minds – that's us and our husbands. Nathan is great! When I'm traveling for seminars I feel his greatness even more! A stable and growing marriage is one of life's triumphs.

> *"Two are better than one, because they have a good return for their labor: If either of them falls down one can help the other up. But pity anyone who falls and has no one to help them up. Also, if two lie down together, they will keep warm. But how can one keep warm alone? Though one may be overpowered, two can defend themselves. A cord of three strands is not quickly broken."*
> (Ecclesiastes 4:9-12)

So I love to buy socks! With five kids, I get to live out that personal joy several times a year. I'm into all the limited time only stuff like red and white, striped, knee socks for Christmas, pink and white heart socks for valentines and all kinds of prints and various colored solids for all occasions. I also love to find huge bargains on athletic socks and anklets. I love buying socks, pairing them and putting them on little feet; especially the ones with trucks or frogs on the sides or bows and butterflies. I hate it when one of our specialty socks gets lost! I can't just go buy another one. Limited time only and holiday socks are gone when they're gone. No open stock!

Pardon the over simplification, but my husband cannot be replaced! He is my match! He is special edition, one of a kind and I don't want to lay in the bottom of the basket waiting for him, nor do I want him waiting around for me – or wondering where I am. This takes planning, focus, timing and consideration. A pair of good socks not only looks nice, but as a team they protect, cushion and keep our feet clean. Can I compare that to a good marriage? As a team we protect our children from harm, we cushion them from the harshness around them and we keep them clean in a sometimes dirty and perverted world. Socks rely on each other to complete the job. Nathan and I rely on each other to do our part as a pair.

Yet, we are also relying on each other for each other. This can get difficult when adding on a personal business. There are times when busy-ness bunches up. When this happens I can get quick with my tongue as I move too quickly through my list. I don't mean that I'm shouting or belittling or abusing with my words, I can just get too quick. I can speak before I've analyzed a situation fully, I can make assumptions and misinterpret and answer too fast. I can even speak with more speed than I should and walk off thinking I've communicated, when the other person is left standing in wonder of what I meant. When I'm super busy I can get forgetful of routine tasks or misplace things, and when I feel overwhelmed I can sometimes become abnormally quiet as I'm thinking things through.

If things are going slow, I sometimes get a bit worried. I may panic inside wondering why people aren't registering for a seminar or if I'll meet even a conservative goal for the month. These and other incidentals of business can affect my mood. That means my husband is affected.

When I've dealt with a particularly trying client, situation or need to engage further business learning, I can lean heavily on my husband for support of all kinds. Sometimes I need his ear, or his thoughts or his arms. Sometimes I need him to quiz me about new business laws or remind me of something on my agenda that I was too frazzled to attend to. I need my mate!

Now, he needs me too. We are available to step in, step up and respond to each other at any time for anything. And we're constantly learning together. We've even bought, washed and matched socks together as we discuss everything and anything that comes to mind. You know that "Yes!" moment when every single one of your socks are matched up and there's not one, single sock left unpaired? I enjoy that feeling and it comes about few times, but I also love the times I find the missing sock stuck to a another piece of clothing or laying against the side of the dryer or at the bottom of the washer; it's good to have the complete set.

Although, Nathan and I are a great match, of two very different socks, we are not a complete set on our own. The thing that keeps us alive as individuals and a couple is our relationship with God through Jesus Christ. And that is not by accident or left to chance. We are busy! Our first priority in sharing our faith is to pray together each day. We try to every morning and before bedtime, but also we stop to pray when tough decisions need to be made, when we have health issues, when we need wisdom for life, business or anything that shows itself to be bigger than we are in the short run or over time. We both function well with lists, so we keep a list of prayer needs and jot down the results of our prayers. There have been times we've prayed for hours, days, weeks and months about the same things and other times when five minutes was enough. Either way we watch as God fills in the gaps that the two of us couldn't have accomplished.

We also seek God's Word – The Bible. We read it to the kids, of course, but it's full of wisdom to keep us knowing, growing and going! We use to do this on a regular schedule until we were blessed with a growing family. However, I don't think we consult with and enjoy it less. At times we run to it! We now have an "open schedule" with the best instruction manual on earth!

I've mentioned our fellowship times with other Christians, but truly the first "other Christian" in our lives is each other. Nathan is my brother, my husband, the father of our children and the love of my life. I love having our friends, family, church groups and business associates, but he is first, foremost and the match to my pair. I don't want one of us stuck in the fold of a sheet and the other between the couch cushions! The best way to stay paired-up is to keep a focus on God then each other.

In business, we are complimentary. We bring different things to the table when discussing options, schedules and outcomes. There was a short-lived fad, not long ago, in which two non-look-alike socks were worn as a pair. This fashion blew through our oldest child's elementary school. He said the girls were into it more than the guys. Well, I'm a girl and I love crazy, funny and bright colored socks. If I were a sock – play along with me now – I'd be a bright, red, knee-high with multi-colored polka dots and Nathan would be a medium brown, fine gauge cotton, trouser sock. And sometimes I need him to be a highly cushioned and absorbent gym-sock, which he also loves. That's when this business girl needs comfort, rest and relaxation on the court!

Are you and your hubby a match made in heaven? I'm not sure I even agree with that phrase, but I know with God's help we can be a match bound for heaven! We all know that anything worth doing is worth doing well and anything we deem as truly important we will put at the top of our priorities. Lots of times our sock drawers are at the top of our dressers. We all love a fresh, matching pair. How close to the top of your day, and life, is a growing marriage rooted in faith and trust in God? When it comes to that extra special pair-up, there must be three in the knot or bundle!

## CHALLENGE

What type of sock would represent you the most? What about your husband? What if you could go out and find that type of sock together – would you? I like visuals. Discuss planning a date which includes sock shopping. What type of sock would remind you of your faith and reliance on God? Find your three socks and bundle one set of them together for your sock drawer and one for your husband's. Every time either of you open your drawer you'll see that bundle of three. Yep, it's silly, fun and may seem like nonsense, but it may also be gripping! Keep your mate close – he's limited edition! Keep close to God – He's the only one!

# Day 14.
# Undeniably Clean

Do you read labels? Honestly, I usually pick something I like then stick with it. If the new and improved comes out, I may disregard its latest claims or new packaging to go with what I know. While grocery shopping with one of my sons, he spotted a product make-over. It was our current laundry detergent. He asked if since it was now new and improved if that meant we had been using the old and icky! That led into a nice conversation about improving where we can, if in fact it's progressive and truly better, and knowing when something does the job very well as is.

*"Have mercy on me, O God,*
*according to your unfailing love;*
*according to your great compassion*
*blot out my transgressions. Wash away all my iniquity*
*and cleanse me from my sin.*
*Cleanse me with hyssop, and I will be clean;*
*wash me, and I will be whiter than snow."*
(Psalm 51:1, 2 & 7)

So, I was shopping with my second oldest son. He was seven. He's my little man with curiosity to spare! It seems he doesn't miss a thing and when something grabs him, he HAS to investigate. He's also the one that came in wearing the squished caterpillar on his shirt a couple devos ago. While we were discussing laundry soap, then dish soap then shampoo, he asked for the definition of "squeaky clean." I said it's when all the stuff you drug in from the back yard is scrubbed off your body and leaves itself in the bathtub, and you get out feeling fresh and sort of not slippery, but squeaky, if you rubbed yourself. I knew what he was thinking – he was gonna try it. What I didn't anticipate was that he'd try it on his younger brother!

When I heard a bunch of yelping in the bathroom, I ran to see who was irritating who, after bath time. Nathan had one wrapped in a towel and another standing in his underwear apologizing for the "burn" on his brother's arm. "He did not squeak," he rebuked as I barged into the room. "Oh yes he did," my husband laughed. We had another talk about "squeaky clean" and put them both to bed.

The next morning was a Saturday. All seven of us went out to work in the garden. We don't get a load of produce from our 6x8 patch planted in tomato plants, basil and oregano, but we get a lot of learning out there. It's our spaghetti garden. We bring its yield into the kitchen as a starter for fresh marinara sauce and I get out the homemade pasta maker.

As we pulled weeds, poked at worms, snipped off yellowing leaves and discovered a couple bugs of unknown variety, we also got dirty. I'm a clean freak. I want my kids clean, fresh, smelling great, good haircuts, trimmed nails and scrubbed behind the ears. That takes some time with five young ones that aren't able to take care of all that themselves. And many times we're scrubbing the bathtub between scrubbings of children. It's an ongoing method of cleanliness!

As I started part two of this devotional I wanted to target more of the spiritual aspects of our lives, because without taking time and consideration for that part of our beings, nothing else works as it should or could. But there's something that works as a constant, consistent and guaranteed benefit to us that we don't work for at all; it's worked out for us. The loving cleanup we receive in Jesus Christ.

In the Psalms, David knew he had sinned against God's commands. He knew for sure his cry for help and forgiveness would be met with love, compassion and a good washing that would render him spotless! He didn't have to do the scrubbing, just the asking. This is how it is for us as we walk out our faith in Jesus. We need to accept this truth no matter what day it is, no matter what happened and without regards to our emotions which may tell us we can't get clean enough to "squeak."

When I became an entrepreneur, I was taking my imperfect self into yet another area that could tempt, test and try me in ways of which I had little foreknowledge. What a trip it was! I made mistakes and learned many lessons. I sometimes struggled with feelings of failure and unworthiness. I sometimes felt dirty from inner accusation and too much introspection. I remember an afternoon, phone conversation with our pastor's wife. I had myself thought into a huge pit of vipers – I would never be the person I had hoped for. I'd never be free of mess-ups, mix-ups, and misunderstandings. I'd never be blemish-free or spotless. And I'd never last one complete day totally clean, without needing to wash again. She reminded me that Jesus is the one who does the real washing; we just do the obeying. We just let Him put us in the bath. She also reminded me that it was His pleasure, as well as His duty, to present us to the Father blameless and clean. And she reminded me that no one, not even one, was above the soil of this earth. And I should rejoice in His ability to preserve me, rather than concentrate on my disability to stay pristine.

When I think about His love and mercy, and His total willingness, sacrifice and good will toward each of us; I feel such relief! He's able to throw my outer self, or the clothes others see, into the washer with a "detergent" that needs not to be improved and He's just a capable to cleanse me on the inside, where it's just me. You and I can stay undeniably clean in Him, ready to face each day, in every way, expertly cleaned!

Think about the many things you must clean, dust, scrub and shine. Think about the loads of wash you do on a regular basis. You want your surroundings to be clean and in good working order. You like fresh, nice smelling clothes and people in your house. You know it's a job with a lot of repetition and maintenance, and you accept that responsibility! How much more does Jesus take upon Himself to keep us clean!

## CHALLENGE

Read Psalm 51. Apply it to any area you feel the need. Apply it any time you need assurance of cleansing and renewal. We don't have to clean ourselves up with methods we've devised. We just come and ask for the bath! We leave the "bathtub ring" to Him as we walk away in a fresh, fluffy, amply covering towel of His love and grace!

# Part 3
# What to do When the Washer Breaks

# Day 15.
# When it Just Breaks

You're standing there in desperate need for the washer to spin the water from an extra-large load and it won't move! It made a horrible sound then a clunk and stopped. Visions or all sorts run through your head. You'll have to squeeze the drowning items one by one, pack them into large, leak-free, plastic storage containers and haul them to the laundry mat to start all over. Or maybe you can call the neighbor asking to do one emergency load or you start carrying dripping-wet clothes to the bathtub. What a nightmare!

> *"Serve wholeheartedly,*
> *as if you were serving the Lord, not people,*
> *because you know that the Lord will reward*
> *each one for whatever good they do,*
> *whether they are slave or free."*
> (Ephesians 6:7-8)

I stood there in disbelief! It was two hours before our family was to attend a formal banquet in honor of a close friend. I wanted our two youngest sons to wear matching shirts and our daughter wanted to wear a special blouse she had worn the night before. I figured I had plenty of time to wash and dry just three shirts. The rest of the load could be dried when we returned home. As I lifted the lid to check out the clunk, followed by silence, I felt sick. I remembered I had tossed in the shirt Nathan wanted to wear that evening. It's not the end of the world if we all wear something else, but having those clothes sit there while we had to go away and then come home and check out the washer, was overwhelming.

I searched my memory trying to recall if I had heard that same sound before during an appliance breakdown. Or if I had heard anyone else describe such a sound and result at their house. I called Nathan's cell phone. I duplicated the sounds and the clunk the best I could and he threw out a couple ideas then told me he was running late. Yikes! I chose the twist, wring, squeeze and toss into the bathtub solution and got the kids ready for the banquet. But I sat through our friend's honor's presentation with a mind half-there. The washer was working just fine the day before. How could it just go kerplunk like that? Maybe you're wondering why I had to figure out all the "whys" about the breakdown. It's because I hate to be caught off guard and pride myself in preplanning and trouble shooting. Rarely does something just break on me.

My husband says I hear things that aren't there when it comes to the car, the furnace, refrigerator or any other machine we own. Or he says, yes, he also hears the sound, but it's supposed to sound that way. And I wrinkle up my nose and say, "it didn't make that sound yesterday."

I suppose with five children to keep things cold for, or things washed and dried for, or taught and entertained, or driven to school, ballet, soccer or little league – you get the picture! I don't do break-downs!

The next day Nathan painstakingly emptied the washer of its overnight water and started taking it apart! Now, I hate breakdowns as much as he likes to figure them out. I don't even remember what he said except that he could fix it – tomorrow. Believe me, I was ready to go pick out a new one and have it delivered tomorrow! But, I waited. Something I've learned about all the machines around us is that they don't heal. They have to be fixed. So, when I hear something, even if it's not there yet, it's about to be and it isn't going to go away if the thing gets a little rest. I'm all for savvy spending, bargain hunting and proper consumer research, but there are times when the breakdown gets me down and I just want to jump on it! This was one of those times.

I did an emergency load at the neighbors and three at the laundry in town, including the one that sat draining in the bathtub. Something else came up and Nathan wasn't able to get to the washer for another couple days. However, he was able to fix it and with grand announcement presented me with a working, spin cycle.

I'd like to say I was so attuned to my early business ventures that I could "hear" things about to happen, or see them before they actually came into being, but that wasn't the case. I had to learn the sights, sounds and vibrations of success as well as something gone awry, just as I had my car and appliances. I remember standing over an email, reading and rereading it. I was completely disillusioned. A client I had had for months was taking her photography needs elsewhere. She had always complimented my work and customer care. She had referred several people to my studios. I sat before my laptop and wondered why I didn't hear the "clunk" before she decided to leave.

That evening I sat quietly at the table. I jumped up to help the kids as needed and answered any questions posed to me, but otherwise I was deep in thought. Where had I gone wrong? After the kids were tucked in, I went through my emails with the departing client. I wanted to understand my mistake, if there had been one, before I apologetically replied. There was no sign of trouble.

Nathan asked why I automatically thought I had done something wrong. He said maybe she's moving, or she has to patronize her nephew's services, or she got a coupon to a department store's studio. He suggested a few other reasons to make me smile; such as maybe she picked up an old Polaroid at a yard sale and now she's all about pictures on demand or her walls are so covered in portraits that she can't get any more until she gets a larger house. But it was the last one that really got me. Perhaps she just wanted to go someplace else for no particular reason and it was my turn to lose a client. I was so shaken that I took my dismay to the Lord in prayer.

I called her - ready to apologize. She assured me that my work was fantastic and that I'd always been timely, fair and professional. She loved my backgrounds, my turn around time to present proofs and finished portraits and my pricing was reasonable. However, she had seen a studio set up by another photographer and wanted to try it out for variety. While I felt deflated, I was also relieved. It was nothing I could have prevented, although I was curious about the other photographer! I checked out his studios and came home inspired. I hadn't done anything wrong, but when she decided to discontinue with me, she just did. Clunk!

It can be hard when something goes surprisingly wrong in business. It's worse when we know for sure that we have served a customer or client well. It hurts personally and professionally. Have you ever been suddenly "clunked" and left to wring out possible answers as to why? Have you been the one to "clunk" a fellow, small-business owner? Everything touches us more when we're smallish and representing ourselves. But that's also one of the best parts of what we do. We're personal even when it breaks down.

## CHALLENGE

Think about a time you lost a customer or client. Did you race in to fix it or wait a day or two to think it over and research for clues? If you found evidence, how could it have been handled differently as troubled spots came along? Remember, although it may hurt to lose a client, it may also be a necessary thing depending on the situation. Just be sure you responded well to the warning signs as they happened. As Christians, it is the Lord we are serving. We would give Him our best in every way, and when we do so for others it gives Him glory. If we get "clunked" it's only temporary and hopefully not often.

But in any case, He will reward our diligence to work as unto Him!

# Day 16.
# Kicking the Machine

Can this machine be fixed? In the previous devotion I recounted a time when my husband saved the day by making our washer spin once more. I could tell him something was wrong, but couldn't diagnose it. I stood there wanting to kick the thing, but what good would that have done? I had broken a toe before while running and it wasn't something I wanted to repeat! He understood the problem and made the call to fix it.

> *"Let us not become weary in doing good,*
> *for at the proper time we will reap*
> *a harvest if we do not give up."*
> (Galatians 6:9)

I'm a lawyer that helps people with the legalities of their business. I draw up contracts that help to protect their interests and advise them concerning the best way to handle such things as record keeping and accounting. I work mainly with photographers and have my own photography business. So, I help them do the same thing I'm doing. My goal is to help them avoid some of the pitfalls I've already crawled out of and offer suggestions that will ensure step by step progress to help realize their dreams. As a business consultant, I also help to diagnose the problematic aspects of self-employment. I wear many hats.

When someone comes to me with a headache and a frown wondering if their particular thing can be fixed, I listen hard and long then brainstorm solutions. I'd much rather exhort to go into business and how to go about it than to stand there before the machine wondering if it should be scrapped or saved, but troubles will come. I wish every start-up was a sure thing! At times I've had to advise to kick the thing to see if "wakes up" and gets back in gear. A few times, I've helped kick it! Knowing that a person is asking me to help figure out something so close and personal is a huge show of trust and I take it seriously. Can this thing be fixed?

I think back to the times I stood over the washer, dryer, laptop or even the lawnmower. Diagnostic testing must be done by an expert! If I thought for one moment that I could diagnose and fix the lawnmower, I'd be the best laugh on the block! But when it comes to small business I'll take a good shot at it.

I've had a few associates who had terrific ideas they just needed a bit of a kick themselves! They needed a little encouragement, prodding and follow-up. Fixed!

I've had several fellow entrepreneurs, who started strong then lost their wind as things got tough with business laws, clientele, cost of materials and family circumstances. A few had set their expectations so high that they crashed when things didn't accelerate at the pace they anticipated. Most of those things can be kicked back into proper functioning.

In years gone by moms, grandmas and great-grandmas darned the repairs to the family's thick, woolen socks. The yarn came from their own sheep or by way of barter. I'm talking a long time ago. Each pair of socks was precious! The time, talent, materials and love that went into them was tremendous. They fixed them over and over. I saw an old pair of hand-knitted socks that had been darned so many times that the repairs seemed to be more than the original stitches! To throw out a pair or even a single sock was virtually unheard of. You might say that knitting and darning was one of the personal businesses of yesterday's homemaker. If they got real good at it, had some spare time and a few extra bucks they made socks to sell for a few cents a pair, and put those pennies back into the business. They didn't discontinue unless they were incapacitated!

I realize we aren't all sitting before the fire with baskets full of yarn and needles in hand, but one thing that is all too easy for us today is to give up when evaluating whether or not we need to fix the thing. We may be too quick to toss the project. We may not be facing the dire needs they did on the prairie and we have alternatives, but when I'm diagnosing whether or not something can be saved I think about the time, talent, sacrifice, people and funds that have gone into the thing. I look at the necessity of the thing, which considers both the product or service and its degree of benefit to the person and their family or community. We don't want to give up too quickly. Usually things that were worth starting are worth improving until a fruitful harvest is reaped!

This is one reason I slowed down a few months into personal business. I wanted to do so many things. My interests were varied and my goals far reaching. But we can work ourselves out of business if we do not mind our skills, talents and resources. A few times when an appliance had broken down, I wanted to run out and replace it. Fixing it takes time and can get messy. Sometimes when we're repairing one thing it brings up other areas we weren't ready to face. It can be this way in our relationships and our businesses. I say try your hardest to "kick" the thing back into order, but you needn't break a toe. Get the help you need to diagnose and repair.

The Bible has a lot to say about patience and it's not something that can be built into our characters overnight! When we see something that could be fixed an entirely new work is begun. Many of the machines around our homes can break in an instant, yet take time to repair. Is there some aspect of your business that should be met with the courage and patience to see it through? You may have to cut back, improvise and adjust your methods while it's being fixed. You may get half-way through the repair and wonder why you chose to revise rather than scrap! Re-evaluating is certainly allowed just do it on a day when others things are working well, including the washing machine!

# CHALLENGE

Choose one, small area of your business that's giving you a headache. Evaluate its purpose and the way you're currently implementing it. Why did you start it anyway? If its purpose is still valid, think of all the ways it can be revamped rather than discontinued. Set workable goals to accomplish its repair then put it back to work for you. Learn to be an expert about your particular business. Read, inquire, apply and re-evaluate. With time and patience you'll be the expert to diagnose each things effectiveness and know exactly when to fix or flee!

# Day 17.
# The Nuts and Bolts
# - Fixing It

When we've determined to fix an aspect of our business that usually encompasses fixing part of ourselves. It can be easier to change our marketing and development procedures than to correct an attitude or obtain more education. I'd rather design a more effective website, telephone presentation or contract for new clients than do a personal make-over, but many times the best change for my business comes from within. Yet, when it comes to that, I still have a choice. Will I fix me or not? I may choose to replace the washing machine, but I can't replace me. That's when "fixing" is always the best choice!

> *"Surely you need guidance to wage war,*
> *and victory is won through many advisers."*
> (Proverbs 24:6)

Let's suppose you've targeted a weak spot in your business and you have a plan of attack to bring it to its full potential. You have the materials, manpower or womanpower, know-how and resources. You have your list of ways it didn't work the first time around and your other list of how it can be improved. You also have your list of why the thing was needed in the first place way back from its inception. Now what? You're the same person! New methods in the hands of the same person can be a challenge. If my washer keeps breaking or doesn't perform at its best, it may be user failure.

This came as a harsh reality to me when I decided to open studio number two. I love to create "rooms" that photographers use for photo shoots. I have a modern living room setup with large comfy couches nestled around a fireplace, a petite, Victorian parlor, a neutral-colored nursery and more. Behind the studio was a grove of trees, a creek, an old weathered fence and a white, vine covered gazebo. Studio number one had its own picturesque backgrounds.

When I started marketing studio number one, I was so excited that I left a few key phrases out of the membership contract. I viewed those who would use it as being as thrilled about it as I was. I thought they'd respect my property down to the tiny, yellow, nursery lamp with the faux, bumble-bee glued to its shade. I thought they'd tell me if they accidently broke something in one of my rooms and I thought they'd pick up their to-go cups and be out on time for the next client's shoot. All of these things were definitely addressed in my contracts, but I found some people needed them to be spelled out more concretely. When we finished painting and propping studio number two, Nathan reminded me to consider a few things I had missed in my previous excitement. Yes, I was excited again! And yes, I about to miss them again!

I posted a few reminders around the property and some guidelines for usage. I was the same me as when we opened the first studio. I was thrilled with my mauve settee and the little, rose-patterned, tea set I had arranged on the side table. Oh yeah! I must protect them!

Another time I had misjudged our activity between September and December. I tried to implement a new service that did not pilot well during that season. I sat up late trying to figure out how to accommodate all my clients. I was exhausted from personal activity and the promises made to members of my studios. I wanted to keep the service, but it needed to be fixed at a less hectic time. I sat it aside and brought it back better than ever; at a time when I was well-rested.

There was also the time I was presented with an opportunity to partner with another photographer for graduation shoots. I liked her style, her backdrops and equipment, but I didn't know enough about short-term partnerships, and my lack of knowledge and experience proved to be a major source of sleepless nights. I sent myself back to the books, websites, laws and a business attorney to straighten that one out and in fixing myself, I fixed the problem. I learned that temporary partnerships are doable and can be profitable, but they need to be done right!

Another time a tried and true method for scheduling seminars seemed to take a quick turn to chaos. I couldn't believe something that had worked so well could fall apart! After careful investigation, I found I had altered the amount of planning time from several months out to several weeks. Things were going so smoothly that I had taken them for granted. I was reminded to stick to the old way.

I did this same thing with our washing machine. I was so use to piling in load after load then happily skipping up the stairs as it went through its cycles automatically. Usually that was no problem, but the times I told it what to do then took off to the store, the school or for a run and came back to find it stuck on a cycle or in need of another spin, I was reminded to check back just in case.

There are many facets to business that make up the whole. When each is pulling its weight, and we are operating with awareness, we can prevent many of the breakdowns that bring us down. When something does come up cracked, clunked or shattered, chances are it can repaired. When the problem is us – too excited, too tired, wrong time, not watching, under-educated, under-funded – or whatever else may lead back to us, we can usually make corrections and try again. I can't say this enough – Get counsel from someone who's been observing and someone who's an expert in your field then work on it. It's victory we want. I will never fix our washing machine. I don't even want to know how! I'll go check on it but I don't want to worry over it and figure it out. That's a job I'm glad to leave to my husband. We can't know it all. And we shouldn't want to. We should choose our thing and let others choose theirs. I'm fine calling in the fix-it man, even if that means he hands me a list of self-repairs!

What have you decided to fix? Do you have the tools you need to carry out the job?

If you don't, find someone who does. Be vulnerable! If the something that needs fixing is YOU, dare to turn the personal screw driver or to change out attitudes. You'd give the same care to your beloved washing machine, just as I would, and we are worth so much more!

## CHALLENGE

Yesterday, we thought about one aspect of our businesses that could use an overhaul. This time list everything you can that may need tweaking. This isn't to overwhelm, but to cast a beam of light on the difficulties. Beside each troubled spot write down the top three things that make it such a pain. Compare notes. Do you see a common thread? If you wrote many of the same things next to each problem area, go after those commonalities. If you repeatedly wrote about fears, find someone that has already conquered those same ones and gain strength and inspiration. If you jotted down lack of know-how a few times, get yourself educated. If you said several things were too difficult, you need to simplify them. If you need periodic retreats to tackle already working methods and objectives, go ask your hubby to plan a night or a weekend away and make such get-aways a regular business expense, so you can come back fixed!

# Day 18.
# Coming Anew

The giant box was out in the backyard. The kids had markers and crayons to personalize it. Our daughter took out a pink and yellow, paper chain and a piece of tattered, Christmas garland she had found in the basement. One of our sons brought his fire truck and another, his box of building blocks. I take that back about the giant box - it suddenly became small. However, it was a sunny day inside and out. I got a new washing machine!

> *"And God is able to bless you abundantly,*
> *so that in all things at all times,*
> *having all that you need,*
> *you will abound in every good work."*
> (2 Corinthians 9:8).

It was official. Nathan had fixed the old washer two or three times and it squeaked, rattled and bore the dents and dings of time and use. It was time to get rid of it. We chose a new heavy-duty, large capacity, multi-cycle, extra rinse, front loading, gigantic washer for a family of seven.

I threw myself over it with a big hug and sigh of relief. The kids were out back enjoying the box and I sat on the step stool with the owner's manual as Nathan leveled the machine.

I decided to throw in a load of sheets and towels and sit there and watch it. I wanted to know all about my new washer; all its sights and sounds, length of cycles, water levels and detergent dispensing regulations. I was having fun with it! After the load of linens, I tried a big load of blue jeans, then some delicates. The kids were still out back. I was so thrilled with my new washer that I hardly noticed that Nathan had joined them as I sat load after load enjoying the show through the circular, window on the front of the machine.

It's not that I have time or the interest to watch every load on a normal basis, but on this first day I wanted to savor the new experience. I had certainly huffed, puffed and groaned with dismay at the old one! I was pleased with every load and honestly, it caused me to long for its mate! The heavy-duty, large capacity, multi-cycle dryer! It's not that we couldn't afford it, but I'm one to hang onto the old until it lets go once and for all!

I put each load through the old drier and folded them into piles for the kids to put away. We are a work-together family and since our children are still in training phase, for the most part, it takes some time to get things done. But, I was so enthusiastic about the new washer that I ran load after load and had several piles for the kids. They were still giggling out back with that box! I had no idea how all five of them were enjoying that one, washer-sized box, but I was getting all the laundry done with a spring in my step that had long since vanished with the old machine.

Several hours later we all convened on the deck for a dinner of hot dogs, carrot sticks, apple slices and milk. I sat with Nathan discussing the owner's manual as the kids ran back to the splitting and leaning hunk of cardboard. They were like kids at Christmas only the box was empty when they "opened" it. They had to create what was inside! I'm like that in business, many times. I thoughtfully open a new, empty box and create what I want that new thing to be! But! I also love to tear into something ready-to-go with an instruction booklet! Or a combination of create-it-yourself and done-for-you ingenuity.

Later, as we put away the eight loads of laundry I had done, I thought about the excitement I had when my dad drug the large, freezer box into the back yard for my brother, sister and I. We were all over it. It was new and fun. We begged to sleep in it, which met with a hardy "No!" from our parents, but we did have lunch in it and breakfast the next morning. Then we turned it into a lemonade stand and we each earned close to ten dollars in one, steamy afternoon. Then I had the big idea of trying to sell our mom's cucumbers and tomatoes from it. That met with a less success, but we bought our own ice creams that day and had enough to pick up a few treasures from the neighbor's yard sale. So I guess you could say I believe in "big-box" business.

However, the next day our big, box didn't fair so well and the kids were onto other things. I was back with the new machine, washing curtains that begged for their turn in the warm, sudsy water. It was still new and I was still excited. A month later it was still new and I was still excited. This same excitement for the new follows me and lingers in how I plan my steps in business and when I leave an entire concept or endeavor behind. The new has refreshed me, although it comes with its own learning curve and we sometimes have to run around with the manual to figure it out.

Over time, I learned that every new enterprise follows the same steps and once those are mastered we analyze the results. My new washer was still a washing machine. I didn't toss out the old one and acquire some strange, new gizmo for cleaning clothes. It's a washer. It has its own dials, cycles and looks but it's still a means for washing dirty laundry. I analyzed its results compared to my old machine. I'm not sure the end results were that noticeable but the quiet, reliability of the new one made for peace of mind and guaranteed start to finish times. I've changed business ideas over the years and added on new off-shoots to the old. Every time I plunge into something new I feel that same energy, motivation and excitement as unpacking the big box. I bring my "colors" to personalize it and it gives me its manual as a friend that wants things to work out between us. The new many times renews, readjusts, reassures and re-launches! The new brings out the "new" in our abilities to create, mold, shape and succeed.

My faith in God reminds me that everything I need has already been on His list and He already knows the how, when and why of accomplishing the thing. Whatever it is!

He doesn't just want me to work, but to do good work. And He provides the way. By the way, we did go back for the new dryer. It does a good work and completes the laundry cycle along with the washer. Starting anew...

When's the last time you really enjoyed something new? It may not be as big as a washing machine but may have been big in your heart! The new has a way of bringing Christmas in May or August of whenever else, because it piles on anticipation with what's in that box, the energy of unwrapping it and the joy of embracing it. My new washing machine perked up more than just our socks, shirts and jeans!

## CHALLENGE

Sometimes the new is met with fear and uncertainty. Think back to your early days in business. What made it so exciting? What motivated you? Did you surround yourself with a completely furnished office or a go get a nice desk and plop it into the family room? The new inspires. Look around your office space. Is it time for something new that puts you head over heels with inspiration? It may be just a new, dry-erase board or a high-end swivel chair. Or it may be time to close down the old business, that didn't turn out quite the way you imagined, but you learned some neat stuff that can be applied to your next launch. New is new on many levels and in many forms. And new is good once we throw ourselves over the top of it in with a welcomed embrace!

# Day 19.
# User's Manual

They say there are two parts to breakdowns when it comes to man and machine. First, it could be faulty design or manufacturing or it could be wear and tear or defective parts. Secondly, it can be user error. I hate user error! I want to be sure that as far as it concerns me that I did everything right! That's why I spend a lot of time on every new manual that comes into our house. I have an extensive file containing use and trouble-shooting guides and have added my internet downloads to accompany them. Unless there's a true "other guy" error; it's on us to make whatever the thing is — work for our benefit.

> *"Those who listen to instruction will prosper;
> those who trust the LORD will be joyful."*
> (Proverbs 16:20)

So, I got my new washer and dryer and sat with their individual manuals as if tearing into the best historical novels around. I highlighted them, wrote in side notes and sent in the registrations. Then I filed them with the rest of my "How to" pamphlets. However, that didn't stop me from wondering about this or that which didn't seem well explained. Sorry, to belabor the point but I really want to know my machines!

I was intrigued with the fabric softener dispenser on our new washer. Something in me thought if I poured it where it belonged that I was losing some of it rather than pouring it directly onto our clothing. I know the same goes for the detergent reservoir but that didn't bother me so much. After several loads, which I sniffed for the fragrance of lavender, I was convinced that enough of the stuff met with our clothes and was satisfied.

Admittedly, I did struggle with the desire to just toss it in but I've heard a few horror stories about doing that, with a front loading machine, and knew the manufacturer must have his reasons. And usually His reasons did not need to be tested by the novice. Thus, instruction guides!

When the idea to go into business for myself first wandered about in my brain, I consulted many manuals, guides, what-not-to-do books and those guaranteeing success. I attended seminars, webinars and read so many home-business blogs that I had ideas to improve about any new start-up, whether I knew anything about it or not. I would read something that seemed an "Aha!" moment in the manual and wonder if it were more just common sense. I would compare methods and wondered if statistical outcomes had ever been rounded up in the end. I found myself wondering why a certain way of doing things needed to be done THAT way and if there were shortcuts or even longer, more effective ways to get better results. I decided to write a few of my own manuals. I began to study business like I did my new appliances. Why this? Why not that?

How did this accomplish the desired result? And what if it didn't? How could I trouble-shoot the thing?

One afternoon, our daughter wanted to put a load of swimsuits into the new dryer. She threw them in then ran out to ride bicycles with her brothers. She came back to damp-dry, not-ready swimsuits. She had accidently chosen the wrong setting. That was simple to fix; just use the machine correctly and we'd be ready for the beach. Another time I tossed in some sheets and one of our sons came running to say it was raining in the dryer! I had left it to steam dry from a previous load of Nathan's shirts. And of course, there's the big hurry, throw them in and forget to turn the thing on at all! All of those mistakes are user errors and easily remedied. The machine just sits there ready to work properly if the operator chooses to set it to do as it's programmed.

I can't imagine misusing the manual over and over so that we never get what we're hoping for. If we want some magical performance for our mismanaged usage we aren't living in reality. I find this in other rooms other than the laundry and throughout various facets of life as a whole, including business. I don't think there's a one-size-fits-all instruction guide for life and business other than the Bible. After that, the specifics must be taken as connecting to the general, over all Word; as in ethics, motives, principles and outcomes. Other than that a good mentor and additional, pinpointed reading works wonders.

One thing I don't want to do is to intentionally and habitually be guilty of user error! I don't want to break my stuff, myself or others when I could have prevented it. I don't want to slow my progress either when I can help it. Another thing I don't want to do is use the wrong manual! With God's Word as my over-all and above-all I know I have the correct method to begin with, everything else must line up with its divine expertise! When I listen to instruction, I have a good idea of what to expect. I like to leave surprises to things like birthday parties and where we'll go for a weekend get-a-away.

Do you save instruction manuals or toss them? Do you save them but not consult them? Do you have a personal library of what helps to run your life and business that is specific to your needs? When I get rid of a particular item I pitch its booklet too. When I bring in a new something or other its accompanying pages are tucked into my file. And I don't mix and match! The old manual won't help me with the new item and I shouldn't expect the new to align with the old. That's one of the beauties of the new. It's ALL new. I don't think I've ever broken something by misuse, but I have down-graded it's capacity by applying the old or neglecting its specific instructions.

## CHALLENGE

This is an exercise I find helpful to keep me focused and affective. I sort and pitch! Go through your instruction booklets and pitch those that are no longer needed. If you donated your snow-cone maker to charity, you don't need its recipe booklet and user guide. If you set your vacuum out to the curb, you can get rid of that 10 page manual. Keep current and know what you own and how to use it. Set up a go-to file for quick trouble-shooting and replacement part ordering. We're business girls; we know a good user-friendly system is best kept updated and applied. This works with appliance manuals, business contacts, suppliers and support people! Know the ins and outs, whether it's how to reset your new printer or where to locate your notes scribbled onto an envelope when you met that one friend for a smoothie. Then follow on!

# Day 20.
# Remembering the Old While Enjoying the New

Remember back in school when we had a substitute teacher or a new teacher took over and we thought, "That's not how our other teacher did it!" Or a new parenting method is touted by our pediatricians, the moms at our play group or on our favorite, kid-raising website…And we say, "That's not how we use to do it!" From youngest to oldest our children are a decade apart. The way things have changed from baby one to baby five still amazes me. Can the old ways be so wrong and the new so right? Is it possible that the new is backed by a very different agenda, while the old was more tried and true?

> *"let the wise listen and add to their learning, and let the discerning get guidance."*
> (Proverbs 1:5).

Let's talk receiving blankets; specifically fabrics and care labels. I remember loving the old, dense, 100% cotton pattern-stamped receiving blankets. Then I loved the new cotton, stretchy-stuff-added, cloth that allowed me to swaddle our little ones without them kicking off their wrapper as quickly as the older, stiffer style. Then I absolutely delighted in the new, light-weight, gauzy weave that breathed better so our summer babies wouldn't sweat it out and become over-heated. Although the three varieties definitely offered their own greatness to the cause of baby bundling, they all carried the same laundering label: machine wash, warm – tumble dry. Easy enough!

I've speak often of keeping the old on board when warranted and discarding it when new methods definitely render something improved; not just new. But is it possible to love and benefit from the old, new and everything in between as if there were nothing else to rival it? I say, "Yes!" When I first became a mom I loved learning how to do it well. The methods worked well as can be seen in my oldest. A couple years later, methods changed again. Did they work well? Our second oldest is doing great! This same pattern follows with our remaining three; new ways, new ideas, new fabrics, same care instructions. Doing our best with what we have is really the determining factor; adding wisdom to wisdom.

Mixing threads, techniques and compositions to produce better receiving blankets is one thing, using them properly is another and making sure they last is something different still. However, one thing remains; that we give our children tender, loving care and nurture their wellbeing whether it's with the old style or the new. When noticing they all laundered the same I also thought that all washers have the same purpose – to get clothes clean. Was my new one really that much different than the old? If I could purchase a new, old one would I be satisfied with its performance the same as when my old one was new? Some crazy questions for sure and who of us has much time to think about such things. We don't! When we need something new we look for the new, not a new one that is identical to our old one.

In the world of start-ups we know they're nothing new. Home businesses have been around since Bible times and big business followed. All of these seek to obtain financial, self-sufficiency and perhaps provide financial security for generations to come. They all sprang from a need, an idea, some hard work and know-how and a lot of trial and error and a lot of incremental progress that took time. Our wisdom is ever being expanded. We hang onto what works and discern forward to add to our former experiences. The old ways meet the new and harmonize!

If we could interview, Joseph, the earthly father of Jesus or Priscilla and Aquilla, who had a family tent making business, we may be surprised to find many of their old ways still hold truth and we could offer improved methods to save their backs! I've had three old washing machines now and two old dryers. I loved each of my old ones when they came out of the box just as I did my updated versions. Was I sad to see them go? I wasn't sad to be free of their disabilities but yes, there were some features I came to rely on and enjoy that the newer models didn't have. But the newer models had more options. Still all of them cleaned clothes well when working correctly.

My mother has pictures of her grand-mother using the old wringer-style, washing machine! She has stories of catching her long, golden hair in it more than once. I asked if that old, in this case very old machine, really turned out clothes that were clean, fresh and spot free. She said they were relatively clean and spot free, if her grand-mother put lots of time and elbow grease into them, otherwise results varied. And as for freshness; that happened out on the close line. I remember when I got my very, first, washing machine. Nathan and I were newly married and it was used. It was clean and ran well and served us many years, but it was not brand new. My older brother gave us their old model because him and his wife had gotten a new one with five settings and the one they gave us had just four. We were thrilled to get their cast-off. I have warm memories of our miss-matched pair! They fit just right in the unfinished basement of our humble, fixer-upper. They rumbled a bit but I knew when they had stopped, so I could run down and get things folded before they wrinkled. The newer our laundry machines the quieter they seemed to be. However, some came with buzzers to tell us when they had officially completed their task. Today, our dryer has a top, loading door for easy hand-off from the washer and a pop-open, front door that automatically invites us to fold the freshly, dried load. I recall the first time our dog walked by and witnessed the automatic call to remove towels. It took him a while to walk that direction again, but our children ran down to see if they could catch the pop!

I must admit I named one of our old washers. She was getting old but did her best to keep going. She had seen us through three children and wasn't able to go much further. I named her Matilda. That was the name of an aging neighbor who lived on our block when I was young. She was wrinkled and wonderful and baked the best pies I had ever eaten.

When old meets new there's a sort of nostalgia! Like wringer meets pulsing, agitator! What if they could talk? I suppose they'd introduce themselves and find they have a lot in common but go about it in extremely different ways. The old one may have been more durable whereas the newer offering more options. There's a time to mesh both, learn the best from each and maybe create something new ourselves that goes out to investors! Well, perhaps that's bit ambitious but then again… Love the old, love the new. Remember the ways both have served!

Did you ever name an old appliance, a vehicle or some other inanimate object? What did you name your business? Seriously, I used to change the name of my first business so many times that my husband had me choose the top three then had one of the kids pull the winner out of a cereal bowl. Whenever I upgraded my services I was tempted to toss the old or add an additional sub-name beneath it. After years of successive changes, I see the first name still best represented my core intentions although I did add a newly expanded explanation underneath. Have you pulled your old and new together or do they repel each other? Sometimes the beginning is just thoughts-out-loud and the updated version is the true collected idea. Where can you combine them? It's sort of like hyphenating your maiden and married names; old and new walking hand in hand, yet distinct in beauty and identity.

## CHALLENGE

If you could rename your business right now what would it be? Have fun with it! Since this won't be going out on a business card you can playfully speak your feelings about what you thought was good but wasn't, or what you thought was great from the start but learned to whittle down. If you went from Jane's Antique's to Jane's Old West Antiques or from Marcia's World-Class-Buns to Marcia's Home-Baked Goods, think about what made that transition. Where have you been and where do you wish to go? As we keep learning and growing in wisdom, we blend yesterday and today to more fully discern tomorrow. The old may be out of sight but not out of heart and mind. What have you mixed together to get where you are now?

# Part 4
# Sharing the Load in Business and Life

# Day 21.
# Up to Our Elbows in The Wash Tub

I'm not sure why but when I was growing up there was no wash tub in the laundry room. We had our washer, dryer, the ironing board and some shelves that held cleaning supplies and the basket that our mother kept for stray socks in bleak hopes to find their mates. In my laundry room today there is a wash tub right beside the washer. All the wash water empties into it and what's left behind sometimes amazes me. Sometimes there are fabric dyes from our clothes and sometimes just plain dirt. And I scrub it out.

> *"Submit to one another out of reverence for Christ."*
> (Ephesians 5:21).

Sometimes I lock onto something and can't let go. Especially if it's something I have to figure out. One morning after doing a few loads of wash, there was a strange magenta ring around the top of the wash tub. I had never seen it before and had to investigate! None of the clothes I had washed were new, so it wasn't due to that first time wash out. I wondered if it were a combination of the orangey dirt from a friend's acreage and the dark soil from our garden. Nathan came in to see me head-down in the wash tub. After his familiar chuckle then playful questioning I had him head-down in the tub too! Wherever that color came from it had also left fibers. Now we were hot on the trail. It was sort of like bits of sweater but also like extremely, fine hairs. A certain blob of the stuff caught our eyes at the same time and we both went in for a closer look. We knocked our heads together hard!

It wasn't the first time we've knocked heads over the years but this time it hurt so much that tears came to my eyes. Always ready with the arms, Nathan cradled my throbbing head against his chest and we began to laugh. However, he's the one that actually sprouted a "goose egg" on his forehead. And now I had him hooked! He actually scraped some of the stuff from the side of the tub and felt it between his fingers then went over to the window for better lighting. We talked about the kinds of clothing I had washed that morning and even sat and looked at them. We managed to locate the origin of the fibers. It was from a puffy and fluffy set of leg warmers – remember those? Our daughter had picked them up from a thrift store to add to her trunk of costume accessories. But they were brownish. After plowing through the rest of the clean laundry we figured there was some reddish, purplish in the mixture of dye for those leg warmers and when it hit water it lightened up and showed itself! And yes, they were new, still in the package before I threw them into the wash. I had forgotten about them.

It's interesting how two sets of eyes can see two different things when observing the same item. Even more so is the unique perspective each brings when discussing what has been observed. During my growing up years I was always full of ideas for what to play, where to go, who to meet and just about anything else that needed to be dreamed up. At school I was a people-person and my main objective was to see everyone have a beautiful life if at all possible. I worked as hard on people's social and emotional wellbeing as I did my homework. My teachers didn't always agree with my methods or perspectives; such as passing around candy, smiley face stickers or notes that said stuff like, "Let's get an ice cream on the way home."

When Nathan and I were first married, I had so many ideas about everything that I couldn't wait to smash them all into our first few months together! What I hadn't considered was that he had his own ways of thinking even about things I thought mattered only to me. I mean I knew he had his own perspectives, intelligence and experiences to bring to our relationship, what I didn't always know was that green jellybeans were better than red and the reason he doesn't like to eat from plastic bowls is because they remind him of when he had chicken pox and had to eat from segregated tableware to help prevent infecting his siblings. Of course, they all got chicken pox, but he started it and his thoughtful mother tried hard to protect his siblings as long as possible while feeding him from a bright red, dinosaur cereal bowl. I still think his aversion to red jelly beans is connected to red, plastic bowls and he thinks I may be right.

When I went into business, he was my best sounding-board for all the ideas no one should ever try! He also smartly critiqued my good ideas and made them better. And when he thought I was spot-on he celebrated my genius – with ice cream of course! When I think of this life, in all its ways to live it and business, and all the ways to do it, I remind myself that my perspectives alone are not the end all. When I use to pass out smiley face stickers to thirty kids in my fourth grade classroom that was awesome enough it seemed, but when a friend and I put our allowances together and bought a bag of 300 stickers we placed them all over the tables in the cafeteria!

With Nathan, I've learned not just to share the load but to investigate and create the load. The word "load" seems like a bad word but the opposite is having nothing in your basket, it's emptiness and maybe even boredom. When I think of sharing a load I think of work for sure, but also things like the meeting of minds, shared defeat, shared triumph, learning about ourselves and each other – all those things that make life, love and business interesting, challenging and fulfilling. When Nathan and I bonk heads we share the pain, the laugh and recovery and sometimes the discovery of what makes a certain fuzz in the laundry tub.

I've spoken of the need of our spouses earlier but I want to look at it more deeply. How willing are we gals to let our husbands throw in their two-cents and see that it makes a lot more than that? We may be the mom, the house keeper or the business owner but he is the counterpart to all those things. Sometimes we can forget we have another half to ourselves that is really another whole person. Sometimes I launch out with such speed and intent that I forget to include Nathan. I don't do it on purpose; it's just that I can get so excited that I'm fast off the starting block and forget to grab my running partner. I was reminded of this one time when we walked into a business seminar. I didn't realize I was walking very fast, through a crowd, as if no one was with me. I turned to see Nathan's frown of disapproval. I asked him to keep me aware of that tendency of mine whether we were walking through crowds or through life. Do you walk out with a basket on your head or one with dual handles?

## CHALLENGE

Choose something – anything – and set it on a table in front of you and your husband. Take a few minutes to quietly observe the object then take turns sharing what you see and perceive. Next discuss all the ways the thing could be used or misused. This same exercise can be used about a topic. Write down a question which cannot be answered with yes or no. Like, "What do you like best about weekends?" or "How could we improve the way we get homework done with the kids?" or "What are the pros and cons of buying a new car, a new appliance or a new lawn tool?" Getting up to our elbows in anything with our husbands can get messy or become a load of laughs as we share our deepest ideas with the one closest to us. In the business of life or the business of business it's best to utilize all ten senses – five from each.

# Day 22.
# Kidz in the Biz

When I first went into business I had plenty of company and still do. I have a resident soccer player who doubles as a mail runner and inventory clerk. I have a book worm who recommends various authors, some of which are actually helpful. I have a gymnast who provides entertainment and drama just in case the day is too mundane, too quiet or too anything else needing extra spice. I have two truck drivers, whom will one day love to run errands outside of the sandbox, but for now enjoy placing their hearty smiles between me and the screen on my laptop. Now, the dog is not one of my children but he thinks otherwise. So he runs with the pack and I do applaud his watchful eye, his willingness to take the kids out back for a run and his furry coat lying against my feet when I'm pulling extra hours.

> *"Impress them on your children.*
> *Talk about them when you sit at home*
> *and when you walk along the road,*
> *when you lie down and when you get up."*
> (Deuteronomy 6:7).

I packed up the kids for a trip to the office supply store. Like most other business owners, I generally order online but I have a bunch of junior executives that enjoy the experience of hands-on, visual selection. I also needed to grab a few items that couldn't wait for the delivery man. I know taking a bunch of kids into any kind of store can give some people the shivers, but unless there's a real problem our kids are generally polite, well behaved and inquisitive in the best way. But that day there was a problem.

On aisle nine there was a new display of back-to-school, folders. However, we were not back-to-school shopping. I just needed a box of a certain type of mailers and some bubble wrap. The problem began when my children started discussing which folders they wanted for school that fall. I was standing just a few feet away with one of our little guys on my hip and the other standing dutifully at my side, holding the envelopes. I saw it coming and was not quick enough to intervene. Three open front, boxes of brightly- colored folders avalanched down onto my daughter's head. She let out a squeal worthy of Broadway then collapsed to the floor in a crying, heap. Her older brothers began collecting folders faster than my tenth grade English teacher. I'm sure these little mishaps occur now and then wherever children go in this world and I manage them with grace – usually. But on that busy day grace had not made it to my list.

I rushed over to help while issuing a mild rebuke and feeling the fingernails of our youngest digging into my skin as he held onto his bending, squatting, twisting mommy.

He started to slide and flung out his hand in search of the nearest safety grip - his sister's hair. New screams. New shushes. New scramble by the brothers. Baby crying. And for some reason I had the fleeting thought that the dog should come running through and trample somebody.

By that time we had attracted a small group of observers; some of which joined to retrieve folders. A couple of employees arrived to help and aisle nine returned to its pristine condition minus a few crumpled folders, which I paid for and ended up in the kitchen stuffed with spaghetti noodles and soggy cracker. Some things just don't make sense in this world!

I got my special delivery mail out that day along with my frustrations. I scolded the kids all the way to the post office then all the way home for a grand total of twenty-seven minutes of mom-madness! When we got home each of my children walked into the house with shoulders slumped and heads down, except for the baby who happily presented me with a staple puller we had not paid for. I rushed around the kitchen to prepare dinner as one client after another decided to call in their special requests. I motioned with angry looks for one kid to do this and another that while I spoke in pleasant tones with each of my callers. I watched as my kids sat the table, poured milk, readied the highchair and let the dog out onto the patio. After finishing my business call I stood in the kitchen with my hands on my hips. I looked around to see that my young, business partners had done all I has asked and more. And one of them had gone out to pull up some weeds for a vase on the table. I was speechless.

I served each one of them with apologies, kisses and extra marinara. But I also received apologies and warm, squeezy hugs. Our daughter explained that she had seen a certain folder she thought I'd love. She thought I could use it for temporary lodging for receipts until I got them into the correct files. AND it was pretty and matched a piece of framed art in my home office. Before I could respond our oldest gently corrected her as to how I handle receipts and said maybe the folder could be used to carry flyers to my next business expo. Our second-oldest son said he saw a sale on the note-pads I regularly used and maybe I could go back to the office supply store after dinner while they stayed home with dad. The conversation around the table seemed more like an impromptu business meeting and the ideas were well taken. I did run out to get those note pads, but I didn't go alone. I took them all again, but this time we had dad along too. We also bought some carefully chosen, school folders and paid for the new staple puller. And in smiling chorus apologized again for the excitement we had brought earlier. All was well.

The next morning, I reconvened my "business group" in the laundry room for sorting duty. We talked about how many piles we had and how long it would take to wash, dry and fold them. We talked about grouping colors and fabrics and about wrinkle prevention and remedy. We went out to string a new clothes line so an old quilt could sail through the breezes rather than brave the dryer. We talked about serving each other and working together, and I told them how touched I was that they were considering the "business me" as was evidenced around the table the night before.

On the days when three of the kids are in school and I'm down to two to chase, love and care for the house can sometimes seem empty! When they're all there it can seem overwhelming. But most of the time it's just right, whatever that may be, and I realize that it takes all of us to run this life, this family and *my* businesses. I want to impress many things upon their hearts. In order to do that they must be brought near and taught and trained and given opportunities to that will mold them for years to come.

What sort of business team is running around your ankles? Do you draw them into your daily business routine and listen to hints of engagement and maybe even teamwork? I never wanted to see our kids as in the way or non-important to the things we chose to pursue, and so far I think we're doing well in keeping them in mind and connected. They are not extras in our lives, they are part of our main, and although we expect them to mess with our business minds, time and focus they can also, as they grow, contribute to the way things get done, and as they learn, become our next generation of entrepreneurs.

## CHALLENGE

If you have children think of ways to incorporate them into your daily business routine. The smaller ones can bring you your cell phone or a pad of paper. The middle ones can entertain the little ones, straighten up family clutter and dust and vacuum your office. The older ones can inventory supplies and jot down needed items, help locate those items in stores and learn how to do online ordering. All of them can make sure mom is not lonely! If you don't have children but plan to in the future, consider them in the big picture of life in business. Are we in business for ourselves or for them too? If we allow them in when they're young, we may be training our most valuable future employees or the ones who will take our ideas on to greatness for many years to come. Open the door to your laundry room for some quick lessons in math and logic, and open the door to your office to let in all your little partners.

# Day 23.
# Good, Clean Friends

Whether in business or life in general, we all need some good, clean friends. Some of us like to have more than others and some keep just one person tight to our sides, while others are cordially invited to keep a distance. As I grew in my role of lawyer, photographer and business consultant I met lots of people. I love to meet new people. And I'm glad to have grown in my "people sense" over the years.

> *"The righteous choose their friends carefully,*
> *but the way of the wicked leads them astray."*
> (Proverbs 12:26)

In fourth grade, my teacher wrote these scathing remarks in the comment section of my report card, "Talks too much in class – distracts others." Her words were true but at least the things I chatted about were happy things, like what I had done over the weekend or asking people to come over my house for a snack after school. I kept my mother busy baking cookies and making peanut butter and jelly sandwiches. And honestly, it didn't seem like any of my classmates minded being distracted! To my knowledge, I had not caused anyone a bad grade and I was generally well-liked. But, my parents cautioned me to keep my bubbly personality in check for the good of my entire class.

I'm still pretty chatty but the topics have changed. When I meet another wife, mom, business person we talk about those three things. Everyone has a story and I want to know it! I learn something from everyone I meet and I tuck those things away, sometimes in the memo book I carry around in my bag.

Life is full of people and people are full of things to share, but not always are those things good to take in.

One of the unfortunate things about this world is that people are not always kind, honest, ethical or caring in the way they go about things. When I was younger, these negative characteristics hit me in the face like a bucket of cold water and made me shiver to the core. I couldn't' understand why people would not always want to be happy and do their best to bring happiness to others. To me, it didn't matter is the person was in your family, your neighbor, your classmate or someone you met in the grocery aisle or at the park, we should all try to bring joy to everyone we meet! As I grew, I kept that concept and ideology for myself, but realized others did not possess the same outlook and I became less and less surprised when people were ugly and hateful.

When I first stepped into business, I attended many social gatherings and seminars for women like me. Some of them had more experience than others and some had a better character than others. I'll never forget a round, table discussion in which four of the six of us had horrible work ethics. One of them thought it was fine to charge clients by rounding up to the next hour after just five or ten minutes in. Two of them lied about costs of materials and passed those on to their customers. Another one made up excuses for not getting her projects done on time and was late to deliver her product on a regular basis. Now, none of these women said, I lie, I over-charge or I am lazy and unreliable. I even hate to say these things! However, they laughed about their lack of good ethics, morals, and people sense. The other woman at the table spoke out in the best way anyone could. She briefly and kindly stated that her faith prevented her from such actions and that she could never treat people with such disregard, just as she would not want anyone to so disregard her. Next, there was a discussion about the Golden Rule and a few jokes that mishandled it. I made one friend at the table that day.

A particularly sticky incident happened when a woman, who came for a consultation, attempted to get me to agree with her dishonest business practices on paper. As a Christian, a lawyer and an honest and forthright business owner, I could not help her. I was appalled that she was trying to figure a way to falsify business expenses. I was more disturbed that she thought nothing of it to try and include me. She didn't know me well when she first arrived, but she did by the time she left! And she never paid my consultation fee. However, it was not time lost. I prayed that my words would bounce around in her mind just as her own had done before coming to me. And I hoped hers would come to a halt!

I hate talking about these experiences! I wish, just as I did as a young girl, that everyone wanted to help everyone else have a fantastic day, fantastic life and now a fantastic business. With no regrets! However, this world is not in the perfect state God intended and neither are any of us. We struggle at times to think right thoughts, to make right decisions and to do right things and if we don't consult the Bible, these struggles are even worse. I once had a conversation with my husband about the need for contracts. What if we didn't need them! What if people naturally did what they said, when they said, how they said and always had the other guy's best interest at heart? And they were treated the same by the other guy. I've sometimes wondered how things ended up when the hand-shake was a man's word and testament! And about the small, generationally owned businesses that started on a peddler's cart and ended up in malls across the nation. Someone was doing something right and reaped the blessings and of course, others made it big by lying, cheating and stealing.

I find it more stimulating to know that I made it good the right way! The challenge to profit by means that are clean, biblically sound and people-loving is something I find personally satisfying and applying strategies that honor, rather than exploit, keep my joy going. I've learned a lot from my like-minded business friends along the way. When we sit at a table, or side by side on an airplane, we aren't laughing about how we cheated someone or plotting how to throw the other guy under the bus. We're discussing ways to bless our families and ourselves by being a blessing to others. We discuss topics and methods that align with God's Word and the Golden Rule, which is really God's Rule, and how to keep everybody happy. The saying, "The customer is always right" is not necessarily true, but the customer is always treated with kindness and respect is unchanging.

When I think through my list of contacts, I'm thankful for all my good, clean friends whether we relate through business, through kids, fellowships or former military pals. There are all kinds of soil out there. If we aren't careful we'll come home covered with it. At those times we do bring some home we need to be diligent about scrubbing it off so we don't rub it off on the next guy. There have been times when I've sat in a seminar and felt as if I have been puked on! My heart grieves to see how some wrangle their way to the top and at those times I come home and toss those clothes right away into the "wash." I discuss it with Nathan to defuse it, sometimes I'm so unsettled that we pray about it, and I tuck it into my mind – way in the back – to draw upon in the future; under the title of "How NOT to do business." Lastly, I sometimes share the experience with my good, clean business friends if it will prove to benefit their personal, alert systems or to understand why some of their clients act as they do. We may not be able to keep everyone happy, at all times, but we can keep it clean and a bunch of us can keep a lot of it clean to God's glory and the good of our families and reputations.

Do you have good, clean business friends? Are you a good, clean friend? The world of business is open to all kinds of "dog eat dog' practices with little regard for anything but the end result. As Christian women in business, we should be known for our different way of doing things. In fact, I believe a clean mind is much more functional and able to produce the greatest fruit. Besides, we have God in our meetings and He watches over the process through to it's conclusion. If you've employed less than clean methods and have several "soiled" friends, now is the time for that shower and to toss those dirty clothes in the wash!

## CHALLENGE

Think through your list of friends and business associates. What influence is each of them in your life? As believers in Jesus, we should be kind to all without becoming as all. We don't want to completely eliminate those who are unsaved or not real mature in their Christian faith, we can be a light that gives them hope, but we must be careful to keep aware of who is leading who. In business, it's always right to do right, and the right we can know is from the Bible. Let's do our best to surround ourselves with those who would help us succeed the right way and to do the same for others.

# Day 24.
# Mixed Load Colleagues

I've already shared a bit about the kinds of peoples I've encountered in business; not all of which were pleasant. Now, I'd like to introduce my mixed load of colleagues. They're all keepers, just as the different types of clothing I have. I love my brights, whites, darks and all the different types of fabrics. They each serve their purpose in my wardrobe and I wear them at the appropriate times and places. I don't mix them in the wash but they look great in my closet!

> *"No one should seek their own good,*
> *but the good of others."*
> (1 Corinthians 10:24).

I have approximately twenty, close, business friends. I'm defining them as friends per the definition my father gave me when I was a teenager. I was always on the phone, going someplace to meet someone and buying birthday cards and gifts with money I was trying to save for college. There were so many people in my life and they were all very important. My carefully, observant dad sat me down for a talk about classifications of people. He explained that there were close friends, friends, classmates, acquaintances, strangers and enemies. He deemed three of my friends as close, three or four more as just plain friends and the rest he threw into the category of classmates and acquaintances! I was sure I had many more close friends and plain friends than he gave credit for and I walked away from our discussion feeling as if I had lost dozens of people in a train wreck!

I have just one daughter and she's much like me. If I sat her down and gave her the categories as I was given she would sulk for days! And no one wants her to sulk. She's the best drama in the house but also the brightest song and dance routine. She's good on the stage of life and if anyone asks, yes, there is a gene that adds bubbly into a person's DNA. She is mini-me.

So, I took mini-me to a young entrepreneur's luncheon. It was amazing to see the talent and motivation of these young teens. They had invented things, improved things, were managing things and were well on their way to stardom in the world of business. We walked from booth to booth listening to their pitches before finding our table. When we sat down my pre-teen daughter brought out all the business cards she had collected and was arranging them on the table like a game of start-up solitaire. She had collected seventeen cards. I looked them over to see a wide array of young executives.

One had invented a kitchen gadget that imprinted stars into hotdogs (or many other things) for Fourth of July picnics. Another had designed a personal, already filled beach tote per age and gender, much like a ready-to-go Easter basket. A few were into photography; I had gotten their cards also. They were launching their businesses as photo journalists by running around their schools taking snapshots that were put into photo-books and sold in their school's spirit-stores. One of them made photo books by category such as sporting events, lunchtime fun, and hall-surprise. The others made them by season. They all had great ideas.

I watched as my daughter put all the "pretty" business cards to one side. There were bake-shop cards, tutu design cards, a dog grooming card and an all-natural, perfume mixing card. She was bursting with ideas as the speaker introduced each young entrepreneur along with his or her craft or service. We were sitting with a couple of my close friends, yes, they qualified as close friends, and we were enjoying the sights and sounds of our own youngsters brainstorming their next ventures. Among our children were a hopeful botanist, a website guru, a coloring-therapist and a custom landscaper!

As the presentations went on, each young-business person gave thanks to the people who had supported their efforts. They were grateful to parents, aunts and uncles, teachers, pastors, neighbors and even the guy at the pet store and the lady they had met at a missionary convention who had brought up the need for school supplies in a third-world country. They recognized those who had contributed in any way to their pursuits. It was revitalizing!

Later that week, I decided to send out some old-fashioned, cards in the mail, rather than email. I wanted to recognize those who had helped and were still helping me along in my own world of business. The more I wrote the more I wanted to write. There were people from all over and my colleagues were just as assorted as the cards my daughter had arranged on the table. I had to laugh as I remembered my earliest and biggest break in photography. It came from a woman who was a greenhouse-farmer and ran a small produce stand. She had invited me to take close up shots of her tomato blossoms, lavender bundles tied with purple ribbons and her woven chain of red, chili peppers. One of my photos was featured in a small, gardening journal. I had also received help from the woman who would become my daughter's, gymnastics instructor, before my daughter was born. She, and the parents of her first class of tumblers, allowed me to perfect my action shots in her studio. We were both freshly-launching and we hobbled along together until we "made it!"

There had been countless others who had helped me over the years and many of them became business associates and clients. As I reminisced and thought of more folks to thank, the list grew as well as the diversity. Some of my colleagues would never mingle together, outside of contact with me. Many had businesses that were rather opposed to each other, like organic vs. non or beauty products verses natural glow or the return to the old vs. upgrade to the new as a way of breathing, but all were appreciated and necessary to my success and I hoped to be the same to them.

My daughter had sorted her cards according to designs that were pretty then by color. We classify laundry much the same. The pretty things are oftentimes delicate, the colors are separated so they don't "bleed" onto each other or gray each other or rub the wrong way against an opposing fabric. In the business world, we get some of those things as well, figuratively speaking, but we also get a camaraderie and sameness of purpose that shares the load and brings the best out of each one!

When I think back to my dad's classification of people, he's mostly right. But! I still claim that more of my acquaintances are at least plain friends, if not close friends, and I love to mix them up in the same basket and see how we come out when blended! When we seek the good of the other there is no bleeding, fading or fraying.

Do you categorize your friends and associates? It's sometimes fun to take a few minutes to acknowledge the array of people and backgrounds that have influenced our lives. Although each one has been created in the image of God, we are all so unique and so needed! The swirl of color, talent, skill and personality brings beauty to every aspect of our lives and businesses. Who has helped you succeed? Was their business anything like yours? Where are they today? Do you seek their good in return?

### CHALLENGE

Consider sending out some thank-you cards to your personal, mixed load of business associates and friends. We sometimes get so busy that we rarely stop to take in the beauty of those important people in our lives. Thank them for something specific, something that allowed their personal colors to come through to bless you. I purposely keep my circle of friends and business buddies mixed for greater exposure and multi-level learning. Yep, I keep those good, clean friends for sure, but even those are of different "shades and fabrics." Who is who to you? Let them know and thank them for sharing the load in the same basket!

# Day 25.
# The Stranger in the Laundry Basket

Ever have an article of clothing show up in the laundry that's a stranger to the house? My older sons often have friends over, sometimes overnight, and there will be things left behind. Usually it's some hand-held electronic device or its charger, and sometimes it's a half-eaten bag of chips or a DVD. I've also rounded up socks and other articles of clothing which raise the question - did someone leave without their socks or why was this shirt on the front porch? At other times I've tossed a load of clothes in the washer by color only; without inspecting each piece. Then as I fold them, I come across an item that's definitely not at home and I wonder how it got in our laundry. These mysteries are usually solved in short order, but there have been a few times when no one stepped forward to claim their pants!

> *"Do not forget to show hospitality to strangers, for by so doing some people have shown hospitality to angels without knowing it."*
> (Hebrews 13:2).

I laid a pair of size 8 jeans on top of the newly, folded load of laundry. My sons wore size 10, 6, 4 and 18months. So, where did the 8s come from? I thought back through the last several days to who had come over and done what? There had been no sleepovers and although our sons had had visitors a few afternoons that week, I didn't recall anyone leaving without their pants! And I couldn't place a size 8 in the bunch. I laid the pair of jeans over the arm of a chair and went on to put away the clothes that belonged. Over the next several days I made a few inquiries and still no takers for the mysterious pair of jeans. They ended up back in the laundry room in the lost and found basket.

The week got busy and I completely forgot the pants and everything else in lost and found. Many more friends visited and other things were left behind, but they all found their way back home. One morning, around the breakfast table, the kids and I were discussing the wonders of whole-grain cereal when the phone rang. I quickly learned the mystery of the pants! One of our son's friends had a pair of his younger brother's jeans in his back-pack, because his mother had asked him to drop them off at another friend's house for a zipper repair. Who knew! The pants got to the seamstress and I had one less mystery to solve, but this made me curious to go through the lost and found basket, which I hadn't done in several months. It contained stray mittens, a woolen scarf, a couple of action figures, a head-band, a library book (oops!), a box of colored pencils and protractor; all strangers to our house. I found a few of the owners but was left with several items and began to accumulate more. After a family of friends had visited with their twin, toddlers, the sweetest pair of pink booties ended up in the wash and a bright, yellow bib. They didn't belong in our drawers but I knew who to call.

The mystery of who owns what and how things get from here to there is mostly trivial unless your size 8 needs his zipper fixed, but still we try to push away from things that aren't "home." Allow me to over analyze, which I'm good at doing, but Nathan says makes me a top-notch, mom and business owner. When we see something that isn't ours we basically think two things… This isn't mine, I don't want it here and who needs to get this back. I have friends that would make calls until every last thing that doesn't belong were returned or donated to charity within a few days of their discovery. We like our own things, our own people and our own comfort. And it might make us crazy if we left something at someone's house; especially if it meant a trip across town to retrieve it. So, we don't like other people's stuff mingled with ours nor ours with theirs. We like sameness.

I recall a time when everything was new, odd, pinchy and uncomfortable. I had visited a business consultant and her ideas were so not me! She put one strange thing after another before me and I wanted to say, this isn't mine, someone else needs to come claim it. Her business strategies left little room for flexibility. Her goals were tight and demanding and her investments way out of reach for me. I didn't see her approach as appropriate to what I wanted to do and I walked away feeling as if I had met with a complete stranger, offering strange ways and I wanted to go home and forget about the entire consult.

When I began meeting other business-minded-moms, I felt comfortable with my uniqueness and my confidence soared. I found something in common with most of them, other than business, but a few were still difficult for my take on life, family and faith. Their ways were strange, and although I was cordial, inside I was saying, I want to go home and do something normal like wipe the nose of my toddler fighting an upper-respiratory virus.

Strange also came by the way of clients. The moment we meet someone does not make us instant friends. I'm glad some of my client relationships are short-lived, not because of any difficulty or dissatisfaction, but because they are strange. Let's face it; some people are just not our people. That's not to say we cut them down or treat them unkindly, but we know our worlds are very far apart and it's probably best to let them stay on their planet while we stay on ours. And we're probably just as weird to them!

However, there was one stranger in my basket that intrigued me to the point that I had to figure her out! I wasn't trying to send her home because she didn't belong; I wanted to see if she somehow was mine. She was at least twenty years older than me, tiny, timid and spoke with a quivering, voice tone. She moved slow, spoke slow and didn't laugh when I did. In fact, she hardly cracked a smile and when she did it was over in about three seconds. I met her at the library. I suppose she fit the Hollywood, stereo-type for a librarian, but she was browsing through a book in the auto-mechanics section! The only reason I was in that row was because I was chasing my youngest who had taken off with his brother's pencil. My little guy grabbed onto her skirt and pulled it over his face to hide. She stood perfectly still, looking at me with an expressionless face. I apologized profusely while prying his fingers out of her clothing. She said two words, "He's cute."

Honestly, I didn't know if that meant he had a nice, chubby face that all babies should have or his actions were amusing or if it was a sarcastic remark about his obnoxious behavior and my lack of good parenting. I picked him up, apologized again and turned to leave. However, she held out the book she had been reading and pointed to the car on its cover. "Car," she said to my son. He slapped at the book as he wrestled to get down and now I didn't want to let him down for several reasons. I was weirded-out by the strange grin on her face!

We went back to our table to flip through the pile of books that had accumulated at the hands of four children. My little guy became interested in a book about kites and all returned to the normal hum, until the mysterious woman came to chat. I learned that she was mostly deaf, that her young grandson was interested in auto mechanics and she was looking for some junior, mechanics books to help bolster his interest. She was also a business woman. She owned a chain of nail salons! Talking with her was difficult but I walked away with a changed perspective and her phone number. Since that time, I've picked up a few business tips from a well-seasoned master. If I had come across her in my laundry basket, I would have said, who does she belong to? She doesn't belong here! But with time I saw she was "mine"; I just didn't know it!

Do you come across strange things and people in your corner of life? What do you do when faced with something new and not real comfortable? I believe God sends people across our paths and us across theirs for a reason. When I first met the stranger in the library, I had no idea she would end up helping me figure out some business difficulties in the days ahead. Although I did not recognize her as mine, she proved to help carry my load perhaps not in basketfuls, but handfuls, and I consult her to this day, usually at the library.

## CHALLENGE

Is there a stranger in your basket that should be embraced as a friend? How did you meet the person? Have you avoided them since then? Not everyone is a stranger that should be kept until they belong, no more than you'd keep someone's forgotten sweater or tote, but many are sent to bring something new into our lives and perhaps our businesses. If you find someone amiss in your "laundry basket" search out the reason they're there. Be careful and kind as you find out who they are. They may be an angel of one sort or another!

# Day 26.
# Where's Mom?!

I cannot draw. My stick figures look like sticks and that's it. However, one of our sons can sketch out a masterpiece on the back of an envelope. Many times when we're dining out, he sits quietly cartooning on a napkin. I have one of his drawings pinned to the bulletin board in my home office. It's one of me.

> *"In vain you rise early and stay up late,
> toiling for food to eat –for he
> grants sleep to those he loves."*
> (Psalm 127:2)

Our house is a busy one. Some days the kitchen looks like I've cooked for an army at just 9am. And sometimes it stays that way until 9pm. There are days things go wrong or things go unexpectedly right, at a fast pace, and everything changes. On other days my plans move right along; no surprises, no hurries, no worries and it can almost seem boring and mundane. When we've been in business a while and have things well-oiled, things can go from chaos to quiet. I didn't learn to quiet myself though, for many years into it.

When we think about dirty laundry we know someone has to do it. It won't throw itself into the wash then skip happily into the dryer, fold itself with a smile and jump hurdles to make it into the drawers. It just sits there and stars atcha! One night after everyone else was in bed, and I should have been, I was working on a contract. I had to adjust its wording to fit my client's needs and preferences. Then the dog wanted out, twice. Then I remembered I needed to sign permission slips for a field-trip, gather up some art supplies and dig through old photo albums to find a baby picture for a school project. I happened past the laundry room and the piles were jeering at me, as they frequently do. I decided to throw in a load since I had to search through photos, which would take a while.

I found the photo, tossed the wash load into the dryer and headed upstairs. I heard one of our sons gagging and sure enough out came dinner all over his bedspread. Nathan jumped up to help. Thirty minutes later, our son was all tucked in with a bucket and I was washing bed linens. I sent Nathan to bed. In my determination to thoroughly clean the bedspread, I over did it with the laundry detergent. There were suds everywhere when I opened the washer. It needed a second rinse. I stayed up.

The next day I packed lunches in slow motion, but it got done and I was thrilled to find that our son's tummy upset was a single occurrence and everyone, including him, we're just fine. Although tired, I got a lot done that day and was up again late. I needed to finish putting together a few photo packages and answer some emails. I threw in another load of wash and stayed up to put it in the dryer. The next day I was dragging again but made it through.

This pattern continued for the next several days. I didn't plan it that way, but the end of the school year has always been packed with activities and those June weddings come right after. I was busy as mom and photographer. My son, the one that can draw, sat quietly doodling as I emerged with a heaping pile of laundry to fold. It was if he didn't see me at all. I finished my task and went to the kitchen to start dinner. He stayed at the table sketching, shading and smearing over his work.

It was my birthday. We went out for dessert and I was presented with gifts when we got back. I got a beautiful tennis bracelet from Nathan and a new fluffy bathrobe from the kids. Then came the homemade gifts. I was presented with a pink, purple and green floral placemat that had been made at school, a painted rock that said – you rock! – and a carefully executed drawing of me. At least I was told it was me. All I could see were to hands and two feet sticking out from under a humongous pile of laundry. The items of clothing were more recognizable than the person laid out on the floor beneath them. We all got a good laugh then my husband said something I didn't see coming. He said my business was closed for three days! What! We weren't going anywhere, but I was not allowed to do any work other than wife, mom and homemaking. I was stunned and panicked. I had so much to do and he had no way of knowing what three days off would do in the end. I had to work. Three days off was not an option.

As I sat ready to scream with fright, he explained. Two of my photography friends had agreed to run my business for three days so I could get caught up and normal. And that included eight hours of sleep per night. My mind was racing. Could they do it? What would my clients say? Did my contracts cover that? Would I lay awake at night rather than getting that eight hours in? Nathan explained that before I actually looked like the picture our son had drawn, he had to step in. I starred at the floor in silence.

I knew he was right, but he was scary right!

My first day off was anything but restful. I caught glimpses of what my friends were doing in my home office and I wanted to poke my nose into it. At the end of the day, I asked them if my clients were ok. They reported all was well and I slept maybe five hours. The second day they didn't come to my house; they had work to do at both of my rented studios. They called around 6pm to say all was still well and I needed to go take a bubble bath and sleep! On the last day they were back and whispering! I hate whispering! I like happy, bubbly, everyone includedness! Again, they reported things were fine and I could return to work the next morning, at which time I would receive a full written report of the previous three days. Nathan walked around with a smile on his face and I was not happy! We got into an argument.

I couldn't understand why he thought someone else could run MY business. And didn't he know he could jeopardize my relationships with my clients, and ruin my reputation and cause me to lose business and this and that and everything else! He just kept saying not to worry and that he hoped I would learn a lesson about sharing the load. But that he meant no harm and none of the things I was crying at him were going to happen.

The next morning I read the report left on my neat and tidy desk. Everything was fine and I had gained a new client. Also a former client had called to compare my prices with another photographer's and my friends made her a deal right on the spot; one that I would have made if I had been running my business that day. Nathan teased that I'd have room to worry if he had called in my friend that ran a dog kennel or vintage, clothing shop, but he had called in fellow photographers; ones who ran their own businesses according to the methods I had directed them to use. But he promised to never call them in again if I promised not to stay up late and jump up early. Deal!

Are you face down with the world on your back? I think it sneaks up on us and then we're down for the count. I can easily get use to something and before I know it, it has become a habit. I can stay up late and get up early with a positive attitude. I can feel good about the things I'm achieving and not notice the hours I'm losing in other areas. How many hours are you putting in? Do you pay yourself overtime while depriving yourself of things money can't buy? It's easy to get caught up in success only to find ourselves thrown down.

# CHALLENGE

For one week keep a log of how much you sleep. Make an effort to empty your hands and just rest. You certainly keep a log of business hours, but do you clock-in for those things that make your life and business hours more productive? As a mom of little ones, I know I can survive as a mother on little sleep. I think we were designed to function for a specific amount of time and throughout certain seasons, short or long, on less sleep than usual, but that's for being a mom. In business, I'm not sure it works the same. If I stay up all night will I be able to function in business? Think it through. Don't wait until something tells you it's time for a day off. That something may come in less than positive forms. If someone drew your portrait right now; what would it look like?

# Day 27.
# Sun-Soaked on the Line

Not everything in business is business. By that I mean it's not all paperwork, data entry, phone calls, emails and the post office. It's people. Even if we stock soup cans or arrange the celery in the produce department, there will be people. If we sit in a cubicle, there will be people. They are everywhere and our interactions with them count long past the moments spent face to face.

> *"Therefore, as we have opportunity,*
> *let us do good to all people,*
> *especially to those who belong to*
> *the family of believers."*
> (Galatians 6:10).

As a photographer I get invited into people's lives. I see their happiest moments like graduation, confirmation, college photos, weddings, pregnancies and birth photos. I've been taken along on family reunions and accompanied one family on a day trip to the ocean to capture just the right shots. I've also been asked to create beauty from sorrow. It's a relatively new thing to super-impose images of loved ones, who have passed away, into current family photos. Sometimes a family that has miscarried would like the image of a little one in their arms or at an older age running alongside them on the beach. Could I call this heart-wrenching-joy?

One couple I had, lost their son at just nine years old. He was an avid reader and was putting together a personal library in his bedroom. Now his desk was cleared and his chair sat quiet. His parents asked for photos that depicted his life in his room. With great care we put together a photo collogue of life at his reading desk. We wiped away tears throughout the special shoot, but it was beautiful and healing.

Another time I was asked to shoot a graveside gathering on Memorial Day. There a family gathered to honor a fallen soldier just twenty-two years old. They decorated his head-stone then stood to pray. I felt as if I were intruding to capture their grief, but that was their request.

Photography has come a long way over the years, both in how it's done and the cast of its subjects. My great-grandfather had a dark room. I remember him very little, but I do recall the "clothesline" of photos hanging up to dry. He held onto the old ways until he could no longer get film for his aging cameras. And all of his work was in black and white.

As business owners, we have customers, clients, patients or by whatever other word they are called – we have people. And they come to us because they need us. I've been talking about the load we carry as business moms, but those we touch also arrive with a load. They may let out a few key words or phrases at a time or want to tell their story at length, whichever the case they are in our circle of influence at that very moment.

As Christian business owners we can help carry their load for one mile, or maybe two, with the love of Jesus. On any given day when I feel my load crushing in, there are many more with loads more burdensome than mine. If they come to me I want to bring sunshine. I want to be that breeze that refreshes their day.

Those early black and whites taken by my great-grandfather were hanging all over the walls in my grandmother's house. Some of them were too light and some too dark. She explained to me the old time process of photo development and all she had learned from her father. His motto was to capture the unseen in his clientele. That could mean many things. He felt a satisfaction in turning a frown into a smile, a cry into a laugh and a seemingly distracted or detached demeanor into one fully engaged. He wanted everyone that saw him to leave better than when they arrived. I'm trying to continue his legacy.

When I was called upon to photograph the farewell party of a teenage daughter on her way to assist an orphanage in Uganda, I had no idea I was taking the final photos of her life. She became very ill while at the mission and passed before the needed medications could take effect. When I heard the news; I wondered. I still had her photos. How would give them to her parents? Since my goal was to always bless I asked if I could deliver them in whimsical way – the way I perceived their daughter. They had let me know they would keep her room as a guest room for young woman needing a place to stay and I had an idea.

I brainstormed for hours as to the best way to inspire the young ladies who would one day sleep in that special bedroom. On the day I was ready to present my work I asked for time alone in their daughter's room. I had recalled the pastel colors throughout and the ribbons, butterflies and lady bug decals still adorning her walls from days gone by. And I thought of my grandfather's darkroom and his care to bring joy.

Along one wall, I strung pink ribbon about half way up and attached black and whites prints with tiny, white clothes pins. Along another wall, I strung the colored prints. I place the 8x10 they had chosen on her dresser in a frame trimmed in a garden theme then invited them in. They held each other in silence then began walking their daughter's gallery. I started past to give them time alone, but they caught my arm and asked me to stay as they silently wept and walked around her room thanking me for each photo. I didn't know they had some long past photographers in their family and they loved the clothesline of their daughter's last smiles.

Years past and they continued to open their daughter's bedroom to young women in ministry. And every now and then I got a card saying how her room and my photography had especially blessed one of their guests. I can no longer hang clothes out on the line without remembering to bring sunshine into the lives of others. As a business owner I have that unique opportunity.

You don't have to be a photographer to being personal joy into someone's life. If you paint their puppy's nails, trim their hedges, bake their cupcakes or do their accounting, you can be a joy to them as far as your contact is concerned. Do you have a regular "thing" about you that lightens someone's load? Do you offer prayer or give a scripture card for encouragement? Do you offer a better deal when someone is struggling or give an extra service? Are you patient when someone comes in with their story and do your best to give them a few extra minutes? Everyone had load and form time to time it can get heavy.

## CHALLENGE

Think of a way you can be ready to spread sunshine. Sometimes something as small as a dish of candies where others can help themselves, or a welcoming sign and face to match is all it takes. Sometimes we can jot down a personal note on an invoice or if we know the client well enough, give them a quick call to show we care. There are always holidays or birthdays when we can show extra thanks for using our products or services and being timely, reliable and offering quality all the time is the way to go. For every brightly, colored quilt soaking up the sun on the clothesline there is at least one more sitting in the dark linen closet. Let's be the sunshine, out on the line or inside our offices.

# Day 28.
# Laundromat Encounters

Most of us have had to use the Laundromat at one time or another. I went there a few times with my mom when our washer broke down and again when in college. Nathan and I have done our time there as well. The good thing about doing all your wash at one time is that you also do all your drying at one time and your folding. The bad part is lugging it in the car. Some people say they like the social atmosphere of the laundry and others detest it. I'm some place in the middle. But one thing's for sure it's a bunch of people with the same goal and working at it side by side. They aren't sharing the same load but each has their own.

> *"In everything I did,*
> *I showed you that by this kind of hard*
> *work we must help the weak,*
> *remembering the words the Lord Jesus*
> *himself said: 'It is more*
> *blessed to give than to receive'."*
> (Acts 20:35)

I was at the Laundromat and didn't want to talk to anyone. I was tired, behind with many things and my throat hurt terribly. The kids had stayed at home with my husband, at my request, and I stuck my nose in a book in hopes that no one would notice me, as four washers with my name on them approached the rinse cycle. The problem was that I had chosen the wrong book.

I noticed a man looking in my direction and I turned a bit toward the lady closest to me. She smiled and asked what I was reading. Ugh! It was one of those rare times I didn't want to interact. I gave her the title of the book and said one or two lines about its contents. She wanted to discuss it further. Then the guy that had been observing walked over and got in on the conversation. He had noticed the title of my book and before I knew it the three of us were discussing learning styles. The woman was the mother of six and the man worked at an inner-city recreation center. At that moment I wished I was working at home instead of the Laundromat!

The three of us had lots of experience with children, although in very different arenas, and the woman sold beauty products. I was ready for her to whip out her brochure and tell me everything I needed to liven up my look. I had run out of the house with my hair pulled into a pony tail and not a smidge of make-up.

The guy from the rec center began telling us about some teens that frequented his after-school program. They were hard and rude and lacking in direction. My heart went out to them but seriously, I just wanted to get my laundry done and go home to a nap! Yet he persisted in telling us more about these boys.

The woman's opinion was that they needed foster care. The guy thought they should to the half-way house nearby and I thought their parents should get some help then help their sons. Then it was back to the book as we discussed learning styles and what works as we deal with various personalities. A few ideas began bumping up against each other in my thoughts and I threw one out; perhaps you should get these guys involved in some sort of business with mentors that help nurture their personal growth and outlook for the future. My suggestion was met with approval and a business meeting commenced. Just what could these young men do? I called Nathan and asked for ideas. He had worked with many inner-city recruits in the military and had unofficially rehabbed a few of them. His first response was to laugh and ask me if the laundry was getting done, then he had a great idea. He suggested that area churches be asked to donate landscaping, painting and window washing equipment to a team of reliable men that would oversee "The Crew." He even suggested a couple men in our church that could help the start-up and told me to give his number to the guy at the Laundromat. Long story short, "The Crew" consisted of nine young men directed by three older men. Their team captain found them work, usually through the church bodies, and they started learning and earning. Nathan stayed connected with them for a while, and after some business and personality bumps, a good work was begun.

Now, I don't go around trying to find a business for everyone to jump into but it does happen. I have instigated a few things at the grocery store, ladies Bible study, once at a spa and once at a deli. The point is that we have loads and need a hand with them, and others have loads and we need to lend a hand, then the world has a load and we can't carry that, but we can show them how to do it then go back to our own.

I think back to the times Nathan has called a "time-out" and set me on the sidelines. I haven't always responded well. Sometimes I've gotten too involved in my work or someone else's and created loads that shouldn't have been. I've been guilty of helping too much in some cases. I think the best way to go is to – know your own load. And keep your load at a manageable level so you have some left to help the other guy as needed. And if others do the same they'll have some extra energy to assist you.

I'm glad I haven't spent a lot of time in the Laundromat, and on that particular day I wasn't up to load sharing, but God had something else in store and He worked through Nathan and me. It's those types of encounters that reaffirm my place in God's plan for business and touching the lives of others.

Think of a time you had an encounter that seemed only a business connection when it was really a God connection. How did the interaction start? What was the outcome? Perhaps you were on the receiving end of another person's reach, advice and encouragement. God uses people. It's good to reflect on the ways He has reminded us that we are not alone. He sees us and sends others to help share the load.

## CHALLENGE

Have you ever helped someone else launch into businesses? Is there someone in your life that needs a few ideas to get out from under their current load to one that is more productive? Many people in our churches struggle financially, they are in need of assistance on an ongoing basis. What if we helped our brothers and sisters learn a new trade or add an endeavor on the side to supplement their incomes? They say if you give a man a fish he eats for a day, but if you teach him to fish he eats for a lifetime. Is there someone in your circle you could teach how to fish, maybe by becoming your apprentice? Pray about it, it may be time to reach out to that one you already know and always be ready for those "Laundromat encounters!"

# Day 29.
# Sharing with God

When we think of sharing a load it's usually a negative load. We need someone to either divide it up, so it's not so heavy, or get under it with us and lift it to a manageable level. But there are also good loads. In business, one of the things we're doing is making money. Some of us make more loads of it than others, but we all have the idea of making this thing profitable for ourselves and our families. The best thing we can do in this type of load sharing is to give to God. After all, it's Him who has gifted us and enabled us to accomplish each thing we do.

> *"But remember the LORD your God,*
> *for it is he who gives you the*
> *ability to produce wealth..."*
> (Deuteronomy 8:18)

One of the reasons we're in business is to make money. We can talk about all the fantastic ways we are fulfilled through our businesses, or all the great people we meet, or how we're expanding or our latest idea to improve our methods, but there's also the bottom line. We want to make money. In fact, the amount we make oftentimes determines whether or not we'll stick with it.

When I first launched, a close friend encouraged me to give a certain amount to the Lord through offerings at our church. She didn't give a percentage or say how often, but urged me to give a "thank offering", so to speak. Another friend of mine, who was Jewish, suggested that I start with a strange amount as my meager earnings began to come in. $18.00. She said in Judaism the number eighteen reminds us of life. Like the toasts you see at a Jewish event or in the movies – L'Chaim – to life! She didn't go into detail, and I'm not superstitious or think that a certain number is lucky or a magic formula, but I thought it over. $18.00 is an odd amount, it's not even twenty! I laughed, but when I looked at what was coming in at first, $18.00 looked about right. I put it in the offering basket. Then I moved up to twenty, then thirty and beyond. I gave to the benevolence fund and the general offering. Then things outside of our church came to my attention…Needs in our community. I gave there. I gave through the mail, gave at church, gave in the neighborhood and whenever and wherever Nathan and I felt led.

One afternoon while at the park, we noticed a family with a broken down car. It was rusted and worn and the family of five stood stranded. Our oldest son suggested we help them. I had no idea how other than to get them a tow truck and ride home. Nathan said he'd go talk to the guy and see how we could help. Next thing I knew they were both under the hood looking things over.

Our oldest persisted with his suggestions. It was a hot day and we should go buy them some water and snacks while they tried to figure things out. We should take them the quilts out of the back of our van so they could sit in the shade. Then one of our little guys said, "Momma, get them a new car. They will be happy."

That hit me like a ton of bricks! Just buy them a new car? Not that I wouldn't, but it seemed over-the-top and our little guy had no idea what that entailed. I watched as time after time whatever the guys were trying under that hood, did not work! We went for the water and snacks and spread a quilt and chatted. They had recently gotten into a new rental home and doing so took all the cash they had. They had hoped the car would hold out for a few more months. The diagnosis said it was done right there and repairs would be costly. My gut churned with the words, "Momma, get them a new car. They will be happy."

At an opportune moment I pulled Nathan aside and repeated those words to him. He raised an eyebrow and looked out over the tree line. "Okay, let's do it," he said squeezing my hand. What? I was just telling him what was said to me. It's not that I didn't want to help, but doing such a thing was a very new thing. Visions of $25,000 raced through my head! We didn't have that kind of cash! I grabbed Nathan's arm and asked how it would work. He had a plan while I had a panic attack. He made a few calls that didn't go as he had hoped. We got a tow truck and he gave the family a ride home, while the kids and I stayed behind at the swings.

My mind was buzzing as they drove away. Certainly Nathan wouldn't do anything without talking it over with me, right? He wouldn't come back and tell me he had made some offer to the guy, or come back in a taxi because he gave our van away, or tell me we driving straight to the bank! He came back and told me we were driving straight to the used, auto lot owned by a guy in our church. We loaded up our crew in three or four different vehicles and test drove them in behalf of the other family. Our little guy in the back said, "They will like this car, Mommy," to each one we tried.

Nathan made some more calls to other Christian business owners and asked if they would like to get in on a blessing! Okay, so it wasn't going to cost us $25,000. We'd share the load. But we would also share our load…the one called profits from our businesses. I breathed easier as one after another of our business associates pitched in. We came up with $14,000.00 in about an hour!

Nathan made the deal with our used-car-lot friend and took care of all the red tape. He collected the money from our friends and a few days later drove the newish SUV over to the family we had met in the park. He took our oldest son and our little suggester with him. The family had been using their neighbor's car and were surprised when Nathan and the boys arrived. The report I got was that the family was so shocked and thrilled that they took the car for a spin right then. And they were asked if they were "Happy." Nathan handled the deal through to the end and I sat thankful and amazed at the ability and willingness of those who had joined in this new type of business venture.

It wasn't the first time we had helped someone, but it was the first that we quick-called other business owners to collectively bless someone in need. And it wasn't the last. From there, we decided to form an untitled and unannounced, Christian, business owners, blessings group. In a matter of months, it grew to about twenty business owners. The only membership requirement was that when any other member called with a need, it would be openly discussed. From there, each would decide their involvement. Sometimes it meant brainstorming for resources outside of the group and sometimes it meant pitching in ourselves. But no matter how each case was brought to the table, and no matter what the outcome, I can say with full heart – it has been a God thing!

How do you give to the Lord? You may be in a fellowship that participates in tithing of 10% or teaches giving as each heart is led. You may do your giving to organizations or through direct gifts to those around you. As businesswomen, we have been given the unique trust and know-how to bring in an income. At first, we may have a small basket-of-bucks coming in and maybe a small amount like ten, fifteen or eighteen dollars is a good start in giving. However, as our load of profits increases it's good to have a plan of giving from our businesses, just as having a plan of growing our business. And the two are directly related!

## CHALLENGE

Discuss a plan of giving with your husband. Chart a course for it just as you would any other aspect of your business. Is it possible for you to start a "giver's club" in your church or business circle? I am convinced that just as God gives us the ability to produce wealth, He also watches over our usage of it, and blesses with more so we can invest more in the lives of others. Who could use a cash blessing from you today? Share your load.

# Day 30.
# Sharing With the World

The world is huge! It's God-sized. Our worlds need to be smaller; woman-sized. I've shared some thoughts about helping other business owners, and those around us, as we walk our daily lives. Now, I want to focus on another opportunity we ladies get in this world of business. We get to share Christ! Believe it or not, sharing our savior is a business too. It yields better profits than what is taken to the bank! It lasts forever and brings more and more sisters into our hearts and into circles.

> *"Come to me, all you who are weary and burdened, and I will give you rest. Take my yoke upon you and learn from me, for I am gentle and humble in heart, and you will find rest for your souls.*
> *For my yoke is easy and my burden is light."*
> (Matthew 11:28-30).

I travel a lot. Sometimes it's just across town and sometimes many hours and miles away.

I've met women from many walks of life. My greatest joy is to share anything with them that will lift their spirits! I'm best known as an exhorter. I'll encourage to go get a popsicle as quick as I will to join in a prayer or to call a potential client. I love to see people thrive by the moment or the lifetime! Life is meant to be lived abundantly and it takes a lot of us to make that happen. Most of all it takes a relationship with God through Jesus.

I was teaching in a seminar in Houston, when the question came from the audience – What was the secret to my early success in business? I stood there with a silly grin on my face as I flipped through my mental files in search of a quick response. I could have said, great ideas with prompt and tenacious follow through. I could have said, the right skills, people smarts to draw in clients and quality services to keep them. I could have said blood, sweat, tears, prayer and a husband that not only supported me but took an active role in my pursuits. And it would be true that all of those things came into play with my success.

After I had looked over the audience I said – God! After that, I 'm not sure what all was said. I know I related everything I had achieved to His grace and goodness. And spoke of my utter reliance on Him to keep going. The next question was, what would business be without God. Now, I was really stumped!

I had to think hard because I had not been in business without Him – ever. They waited for my answer.

The only thing I knew was to say the opposite of what I knew. In other words, I was gonna guess! I said without

God, I may not want to get up in the morning, because I couldn't be certain there was any point to the toil of life. Without Him, the repetition of breakfast, lunch dinner, laundry, bill paying, schools, doctors and phone calls would be just something that takes my time and energy. If He were not in the picture, I may make huge mistakes with people and finances and perhaps even choose a business that was not honorable. I may not maintain a good work ethic or moral code. I may use people to get to the top or walk away too quickly when it seemed I was at the bottom. I had to think out loud to answer the question. As I rambled away, one of the participants raised her hand. Great! I was gonna be stopped in my search for a good answer. I hoped her question, or response, was one that could be answered in five words or less!

She simple said, I want to know God like you do. The entire room was silent. I stood there feeling as if God had put before me the greatest opportunity to touch the life of another. But! Did I stand there and give over the plan of salvation to the whole crowd? Did I ask her to explain what she meant? Did I invite her to talk with me after that session? This is when my heart is praying faster than my mouth can answer. I decided to continue with further questions and offer to discuss her statement further with anyone who wanted to hang out for coffee afterwards. Four women stayed.

I shared from my heart all I could about my relationship with God and how that affected my entire outlook on life and eternity. I said that to represent Him in all I do was the greatest privilege of all and the best way I could advise anyone concerning life, business and heaven. One of them asked me to pray with her. The others stayed to listen and asked for additional resources. Excitedly, I called Nathan. He congratulated me on being busy about the greatest business of all – my Father's business!

As I walked down the hall to my hotel room that evening, I knew I had participated in the single, most wonderful introduction of two parties I could ever achieve – God and one of His children! If I were to help anyone with their business, in a lasting way, I should ask something about their faith and hope it led to a s discussion about the love of God and His plan for their lives. I decided to add more to the topic of faith in my presentations.

When I got back home, I sat cross-legged on the floor joining the family in the great, laundry-fold. The baby sat in my lap and "helped" as we all discussed my adventures in Houston. Nathan expressed his pride in the woman I am and my abilities and sincerity. He congratulated me for the sensitivity and courage I had when answering the woman in my workshop, and for meeting with her and others later on. My smile was wide as I helped our daughter fold her shorts and tops. Our oldest said he liked to brag about his "business mom" at school, and he thought I should offer some free consultations to some of his friend's mothers. Which I did.

As we finished up with the folding and each one started toward their rooms to put things away, our of our little guy asked, "Mommy are you happy?" I squeezed him close and gave him a resounding, "Yes!"

Nathan had to bring in the punch-line: "Especially when she's matching her pink socks with your green ones." I looked down to see what I was doing. Indeed, I was so happy that I had paid no attention to what I was doing! But sometimes that was okay. I would be on point another time and I hoped that would be while connecting a woman with the One who truly carried their loads and made her burdens light!

How is it with you and God? Have you invited Him into every area of your life and business? If not, why not? Think over your life – your relationships, decisions, finances, health and business. I can't imagine not having Him at the center of life's joys and sorrows. He gets us our family through every test and trial and adds additional meaning to our times of rejoicing! Who gets you through and with who do share your triumphs? Who gets the credit for you success and the stabilizer when things get crazy?

## CHALLENGE

If God is not part of your life and business I urge you to connect with Him. That's the greatest piece of advice and most important way I can direct you to wholeness and rest. We may have spouses, children and extended family; we may be surrounded by business associates and clients – but the true fellowship with others starts with true fellowship with Him. Get connected! He wants you in His corporation! Make the best business contact you could ever make. Call upon Him – maybe even over the laundry basket – He's waiting to share your load!

# In Conclusion

We've plowed through 30 days of Dirty Laundry together! And there will be many more just like these. We'll over-extend ourselves, get impatient, yell, cry, lose and forget things, feel lonely, make mistakes, not know how to proceed and fell like quitting. We'll also make calls, meet for coffee, find help, exercise gratitude and savor the small achievements as well as the large. Lastly, we'll spread our love, joy, helps and healing and the reason for our hope. We are women in businesses of all kinds and one of our greatest assets is each other! Find at least one business-gal to share with on a regular basis. Pray together, discuss together and have fun together. We don't have to be alone; there are a lot of us out there. And even on the worst of wash days - WE GOT THIS!

Made in the USA
San Bernardino, CA
13 November 2017